The 5-Minute Marketer

395 Ways To Market Your Business In Just 5 Minutes

By Stefan Ekberg

HARRIMAN HOUSE LTD
3A Penns Road
Petersfield
Hampshire
GU32 2EW
GREAT BRITAIN
Tel: +44 (0)1730 233870
Email: enquiries@harriman-house.com

Website: **www.harriman-house.com**

First published in Great Britain in 2014
Copyright © Harriman House 2014

The right of Stefan Ekberg to be identified as the Author has been asserted in accordance with the Copyright, Design and Patents Act 1988.

ISBN: 9780857193902

British Library Cataloguing in Publication Data | A CIP catalogue record for this book can be obtained from the British Library.

No responsibility for loss occasioned to any person or corporate body acting or refraining to act as a result of reading material in this book can be accepted by the Publisher, by the Author or by the Employer(s) of the Author.

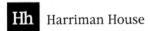 Harriman House

Contents

Follow us, like us, email us

@HarrimanHouse

www.linkedin.com/company/harriman-house

www.facebook.com/harrimanhouse

contact@harriman-house.com

Free eBook version

As a buyer of the print book of *The 5-Minute Marketer* you can now download the eBook version free of charge to read on an eBook reader, your smartphone or your computer. Simply go to:

http://ebooks.harriman-house.com/5minmarketer

or point your smartphone at the QRC below.

You can then register and download your free eBook.

About the author

Stefan Ekberg has worked in marketing for small business for 20 years and has written approaching 30 books on how small business owners can market themselves with limited resources. Every week some 230,000 subscribers receive his newsletter about marketing. He also runs Redaktionen, Sweden's hottest publishing company for entrepreneurs (**www.redaktionen.se**). In 2012 Stefan was nominated for the Entrepreneur of the Year award in Stockholm.

As a small business owner for two decades Stefan has encountered all the problems small businesses are up against and is well known in Sweden for showing small businesses the shortcuts to business solutions.

Stefan is also a business journalist and spent time as head writer at several major Swedish television soap operas earlier in his career.

Introduction

STOP!

Get a pen before reading on.

This book is packed with ideas for the small business owner who wants to get ahead of the competition. I'm talking about you of course. You'll need a pen so that you can make notes as you go. At the back of the book there is space for you to make a list to help you organise your ideas and decide which ones you want to work on.

Whenever you read an idea that you like go to the back of the book and write down the number of the idea so it will be easier to come back to it later. Of course you can also underline, circle or tear out – anything to create a list using the tips and rank them according to how important they feel to you. Then you can set aside time to work through your list, until you have completed all of the ideas.

If you are reading the eBook then have a word processing document open as you read the book so you can jot down ideas, or make notes in a blank email.

Fast results

This book is perfect if you want things to happen quickly. All the ideas are designed to get fast results and they are all proven to work. They are just the sort of things that it is so easy to forget in the heat of running a business day to day, so this is a book with ideas but also reminders of all the things you can do to make stuff happen.

Some of these ideas you may already know about, while others might come as a surprise. The book is meant to both remind you of the old and to help you come up with something new. Read it with an open mind and highlight the ideas you would like to try and you'll save some time right from the start.

In order for this book to work as a useful tool for you, it's important that you prioritise what you want to do first. I suggest that you grab that pen and grade the tips that interest you in this way:

1. This we have to do right away!
2. Interesting, this is something we have to try.
3. This is something we'll do when we find time for it.

My recommendation is not to do the most important things first, but instead to do the ones that you will find most rewarding. You will then find the contents of this book far more pleasant than if you just see reading it and carrying out the ideas as a chore. So look for the fun things, the ones that make your heart beat just a little faster, and get going with those first.

Let's get started!

Part 1

80 Simple Ways To Give Your Business A Boost Today

1. Let's make a flying start to your day – don't just sit there lazily looking through a newspaper in the morning. Be alaert for something in the news that annoys you or that you have a different idea about, and where you can find some connection to your own line of business. Why don't you email the journalist who wrote the article and let them know?

> **"**Hello Mark!
>
> **"**I was very excited to read your article on X this morning and there's a lot in it that's very good. There were a few things though that should have been mentioned but weren't… [Give your angle on it]. If you want to hear more you are more than welcome to call me.**"**

Hit send and then get to work.

2. On your way to work spend five minutes thinking about how you can sell more today. Learn to live with this phrase: "How can I sell more today – where are the lowest hanging fruit?"

3. Hold a meeting with your employees – it should only take five minutes at the most to come up with a reason for why a newspaper should write about you this week. If you don't have any news to offer right now, what new ideas could you come up with? Tick tock, five minutes is all you get to come up with smashing new ways to give the newspapers something to write about.

4. Look through your business cards and other sources and find ten people or businesses that could possibly become your customers but aren't yet. Come up with a reason why those ten should buy from you now. What have you changed? If you haven't changed anything recently then that could serve as a reason to contact them – why have you maintained your practices? Maybe you'll even make some changes to your business just so you can tell them about it.

5. Send an email to your co-workers and ask them to write down the five most important questions that customers ask them. The idea behind this is to eventually create a FAQ page on your website where these common questions are answered. It takes one minute to write to your co-workers and then you use the most talented writer in your workforce to write the answers to the questions. This also makes it easy for all employees to have a quick answer to customers' most important questions and for customers to find out the answers to their questions directly from your website.

6. Which bloggers are writing about your field of work? Shamelessly send them free products. Surprise them with a package of things today and hope that they will write about them.

7. What do your customers see that doesn't have your web address written on it? Write it there – or make plans to write it there. If you have a product, make plans to print your web address either directly on to the product or make a sticker with your web address on to attach to the product.

8. Ask someone who sells products that complement your own if they want to include your product in their range – and you will of course do the same for them:

"Hello Ellen,

"My company sells XXX, which seems to perfectly complement your product Z. I believe that we could help each other get more business if we sold each other's products. Would you like to get together and talk about maybe working together? I'm free on [give a fixed date and time]."

---

9. If you are not already a member of something that you really ought to be a member of (your local market association, sector union, etc.) then join right now.

10. Run a five-second test. Have a few people look at a certain page on your website for five seconds. Ask them later what they remember about that page. If they don't remember the things that you want them to, then this is a valuable lesson that you may need to change some of your content or make your message clearer.

11. Change your shipping costs. If you can't offer free shipping, try ridiculously cheap shipping and offer free shipping when a customer's order exceeds a certain sum. In my publishing company, we started by charging £5 for shipping, which results in a loss, however we get the money back through increased sales. For orders over £99 our customers get free shipping.

12. Write a note on why customers should pick your company over your competitors. Don't just write some generic stuff about "better customer service." Really get into exactly why you have better customer service; things that your customers might not even know about, but would appreciate if they were made aware. If you don't have anything like that then you need to get it. Make sure your whole organisation is aware of it.

13. Write down your goals for marketing this week. Make sure you have all these goals checked off the list by Friday.

14. Go right now to your website statistics and find out which pages get the most traffic. Put a box for newsletter subscriptions on those pages. This way you will catch most of the visitors that aren't ready to buy just yet. This is especially useful if you sell services, because the visitors will want to check up on you before they buy. If you get their email addresses you will have the chance to get your foot in the door and show them what you're about by sending them your newsletter, ensuring that when the need for your services does arise they will come to you instead of your competitors.

Where you include the box for newsletter subscriptions add a description to explain exactly what subscribers will get if they subscribe to your newsletter. For example, how often it comes, how easy it is to quit the newsletter and what you are going to do with their addresses.

Perhaps create a separate list of addresses of those who want to receive your "special offers" or notifications of sales by email. Imagine what can be achieved with such a list. Say you have 5000 customer email addresses and to send something to all of them costs less than it would to post a single letter. You can do this with a few clicks of a button as often as you think the customers want it. Direct messages relating to this service to a dedicated email address, e.g. offerlist@yourcompany.com.

15. Spend five minutes working on that risk-filled, dream project which you aren't sure will ever amount to anything. You have one of those – we all have one. If you put in small amounts of time towards that project every now and then, the risks will not be as big as if you sacrificed an entire week for something that you are unsure will ever work.

16. Call a friend who will pretend to be overly negative towards you and try out your sales pitch on him or her. Ask them to use all the counter arguments they can think of and let yourself be properly grilled, rebuffed, maybe even mocked. This helps you to fine-tune your arguments and also to realise that you will encounter impolite, sometimes even nasty people, and you need to be able to shake that off. Selling is tough but if you can grow a thicker skin you are on the way to a thicker wallet.

17. Ask a few of your current customers if they have any questions about your products/services. The key here is to get them to reveal things they were wondering about. They might also reveal any future plans they have to which you could contribute your knowledge and make it easier for them.

18. Call a customer that you lost and ask them why they chose another supplier. You will get some very valuable information that you would have missed out on if you just sat in a corner grumbling about being unfairly treated. The customer may never come back, but at least you know why. And besides, the fact that you called will leave an impression. After a while you can send them a letter entitled "We're looking forward to you being our customer once again" along with a generous discount.

19. Buy a few lottery tickets and send these attached to your letterhead to some of your customers. Make a note to call them later and ask if they won anything.

Also, if someone does something well, be it a supplier or a customer, you now have something to reward them with. You are showing appreciation of other people's good work. Tell your employees that whenever they've made a mess of something, they can send a lottery ticket as a little compensation to the customer.

20. If you sell through a distributor include a warranty card with the product that customers can fill out and send back to you. The warranty is of course effective immediately when they purchase, but this technique is used by companies to obtain direct addresses for their customers. If you can get these details you won't be as dependant on your relationship with the distributor to get access to your customers. The distributor may one day choose not to stock your product any more but hopefully by then you will already know who buys your products. There's nothing better than a database full of your customers' details.

21. Call a newspaper that you would really like to advertise in but you suspect is too expensive. Ask how much an advertisement would cost. When you know the price, offer to put in an ad for half of that sum (or even a third). Advertising prices are rarely carved in stone. This is good to keep in mind for the day when you really do need to advertise.

22. Write a letter to your best customers with the message:

> "Everyone who provides us with names of companies or individuals that could benefit from knowing about us gets a present today."

23. The best question in the world to ask yourself about anything you have to do is: Is it worth my time? If you let it become a habit, you will find this question popping up automatically and you will be forced to consider if the task ahead is really that important.

Other good questions to ask yourself are:

- Is what I'm doing really a priority?
- Is what I'm doing going to increase my earnings?
- Am I getting closer to my goals because of doing this?
- Am I doing someone else's job? If it's not someone else's job, could it become someone else's job so that I can do more important things?

24. Show your marketing materials – brochure, website, product sheets – to your mother to see if they stand up to the mother-test. If your own mum doesn't fully understand the content, there is a good chance that many of your customers won't either.

25. What annoys you in your line of work? Write up a rough draft for an article about this with a view to having it published in a magazine for your business sector.

26. Create a newsletter within your area of expertise – but do it risk free. Start out by putting a note on your website saying:

> "Subscribe to our newsletter for tips on nicer looking bathrooms/better salary negotiations/happier children (or whatever you are an expert at), for free."

Ask everyone who wants to be part of this to send an email to you, including a keyword in the subject line. You can start a couple of lists in different areas and see which one gets more subscribers. This will give you an indication of what to focus on in your future newsletters.

27. Advertise with Google AdWords. It takes five minutes to get started (**adwords.google.com**).

28. If you have a physical store or you're at an event put a bowl somewhere for people to leave their business cards. Also, leave out a notebook where those who don't have a business card can write down their contact details. Even if you don't have a store, you could create a *virtual bowl* on your website.

Once a month, have a lottery among those who entered their business cards and present a prize. Send an email to everybody that didn't win telling them that unfortunately they weren't picked, but as some small compensation you have a voucher on your website that they can print and use the next time they buy from you (don't forget to restrict the time in which the voucher can be redeemed). You can add these new contacts to your newsletter mailing list.

29. Surf the web and look for sites that rank in the top five for keywords that describe your own business. Think about what you can do to get them interested in linking to you/working with you.

30. If you sell your own products add a section to your website explaining that you're always looking for distributors.

31. Try a more aggressive approach on why customers should subscribe to your newsletter on a specific page on your website. Then start to measure the results for how many new subscribers you get depending on what reasons you give for subscribing. You can, for example, write:

> "Stay updated on X by getting free tips every week" and vary it with "Right now we are giving away 100 free subscriptions for our newsletter."

Try out different things – anything you think your customers could respond to.

32. If you don't want to start your own newsletter then it's worth taking a look at existing newsletters sent by others in which you could place advertisements. The advantage is that these newslatters are already known to the subscribers. The best part is that you get a lightning-fast response to ads. You can get responses from the moment the newsletter is emailed to its distribution list.

33. Register at popular websites, blogs or forums that relate to your business and where people can leave comments or posts. Every morning, spend five minutes on each site and make a comment about something.

Use your web address in your user signature or name (you know, where people usually put something like "The day trader" or "Wayne from Idaho"). Or add a link to your website at the end of your comments.

If you write good, positive comments the chances are that people who like what you say will also visit your website. It's important to not simply write that people should visit your site or to advertise in a blatant way. A genuinely helpful post is the best type of advertisement for you and your business.

People who use others' blogs to advertise themselves are short-sighted and they underestimate other people's intelligence. Instead, make people curious about you and want to find out about your business for themselves.

34. How can you minimise the risk around purchases? The top reason why customers don't want to buy is that they are unsure if they're doing the right thing. You can remove this hesitation by clearly offering the customer a guarantee that you'll give them their money back within 60 days if they're not happy with your product. Don't worry that all of them will suddenly start returning your products. First of all, you sell good quality stuff. Second of all, the customers will soon forget about the guarantee, since they really did want to buy your product after all – they were just unsure about making the purchase.

35. If you don't have your own search function on your website, get one free from Google (**www.google.com/cse**).

36. Spend one minute linking your Facebook and Twitter accounts so that your posts on Facebook are also added to Twitter. You can do this at: **www.facebook.com/twitter**. And also make your tweets visible on Facebook by linking your Twitter account to your Facebook account (**support.twitter.com**).

37. Set up an account with a press release service today – it takes five minutes and will remind you to write press releases more often. A good site to use is 24-7PressRelease (**www.24-7pressrelease.com**).

38. Create an account with a free email service and sign up for your competitors' newsletters right now. This is of course a way to keep an eye on what your competitors are up to without them knowing.

39. Make a rough draft for a marketing plan in five minutes. Marketing plans don't need to be comprehensive for you to generate some good ideas.

It's all about thinking spontaneously and using the part of you that already understands your business and knows what it needs. The goal is to stop censoring yourself and get at least one good idea out of the exercise. Here are the steps:

- **60 seconds – Think about your product/service.** What can you do right now to improve the quality of your product/service? What other products/services could you offer that customers would appreciate?

- **60 seconds – Think about your prices.** What can you do right now to cut your prices without the quality of the product/service being affected? What offers can you afford to have in order to catch new customers and strengthen the loyalty of your old customers?

- **60 seconds – Think about your distribution.** What can you do right now to reach other customers, or to reach your present customers in a new way?

- **60 seconds – Think about marketing.** In what ways could you reach out to the market that would be worth the cost?

- **60 seconds – Think about yourself and your customers.** What is your relationship to your customers? Do they feel what you feel? How can you show them they are important to you?

How did it go?

Did one thing come up that you would love to try? Then all you have to do now is get going. This exercise is quick for a reason – so that you can disconnect your brain a bit, let go for five minutes, and see the truths that you already know about but haven't yet acted on.

40. Offer customers *buy two and get the third for free*. If you can sell your products in this way you will motivate your customers to buy more. When online, this little surprise is best saved until the customer is about to check out. Make it easy for him/her to just check a box to buy more.

41. Order your competitors' annual accounts for the year so you can see how they have been performing financially. You can do this in the UK through Companies House (**www.companieshouse.gov.uk**) or by using a service such as Company Check (**companycheck.co.uk**).

42. Find the enthusiasm for whatever you offer. One of the best ways is to make a list with amazing benefits that will apply to any and all who buy from you. Find out what your customers think is good about your product/service and add that to your list. Hang the list on your wall or keep it folded in your pocket so that you will notice it often. Your self-confidence and that of your team will be boosted by this list.

43. Write down five things you would really like to know about your future customers. Memorise the questions so that you can ask them when you meet.

44. If you have dusty old products that are just sitting in storage, start a contest on your website and tell all your customers about it.

For example, ask them to submit a photo of someone using your product, or ask quiz-style questions about content on your website. Let them compete away your stock.

45. What newsletters do you read and like? Send an email to them and ask how much it would cost you to advertise with them. Try advertising online in places that you like yourself – there's a good chance that a lot of other people like these places too.

46. If you have a newsletter, make sure that it is perfectly clear to people what they get if they choose to subscribe to it. Most websites fail to do this and only write "Subscribe to our newsletter." Confronted with this, visitors will ask themselves why they should do that, so provide them with an answer to this question.

47. If you don't have a Facebook account get one. It's a little annoying with Facebook because there are no borders and your old friend *Pete the prankster* who loves to remind you that you did this and that at a crazy party once may post something about you that may be seen by all of your contacts – including your important clients if they are in your *friends* list.

This means you have a decision to make about whether you use your personal account socially, to catch up with friends, or for business. I've personally chosen to keep my Facebook account strictly professional and I keep in touch with friends via other channels.

48. Bookmark your sector magazine's website. Make a habit of reading it for five minutes every day. If your sector doesn't have a dedicated magazine or website then maybe you should start one.

49. Allocate five minutes every morning to checking the statistics for your website. The information that you get from your statistics (number of visitors, most popular pages and where they enter and leave your site) could be essential to the running of your business.

50. If you have a minimum order requirement on your website – for instance, to make shipping more economical – get rid of it. Seriously, if a customer wants to pay £20 for your product and an extra £13 for the shipping then that should be their choice.

51.   Put a message on your website saying:

> "Free consultation via email – send in your questions and we will answer you in X hours on your question about Y (your special area of expertise)."

This is a good way to make it easy for people to contact you and you get the chance to show what you're all about.

52.   Send out a letter to your top ten customers and ask them what they think is the best thing about your product. Also, give them a little something for their trouble.

Write something like this:

> "Hello Pete,
>
> "Right now we are doing a quick customer survey and we would like to know what you think about X. How has it helped you with Z? I know your time is limited and as a small compensation we will send you a free present in the post.
>
> "All the best... etc."

Later on when you get the answers, send them a new letter:

> **"**Thank you for your reply. We are now sending you a present to show our gratitude for your help. Is it all right with you if we put part of your answer as a reference on our website? In that case we were considering writing... [here you put in their nice words].**"**

And there you go; you now have a customer reference to put on your website. Fast and easy.

53. Write a handwritten note to someone you've recently met. In this time of emails and cold impersonal contacts your handwritten letter will really stick out. Buy a range of cards of different kinds along with some nice postage stamps and let them sit on your desk so that they are within reach when you need them.

54. Call a potential customer right away and see if he/she wants to become an actual customer.

55. Make copies of an exciting article from this morning's newspaper and send it with a handwritten note to some of your customers, or to a potential future customer.

56. Order something nice to send to someone who has recently helped you with something important.

57. I have had a little 'advert' running for a long time now that has drawn over 3000 visitors per month to my satellite site about starting a business (**www.starta-eget.se**). I put an ad on a classifieds site similar to

craigslist.org, offering my website for sale at the price of one million dollars.

Fraud? Nope. If someone offers me that sum for the site I would most definitely consider selling it, but for now the traffic rushes in. Some people email me asking if I'm insane to think that I'll get a million dollars for a website. Others understand exactly what I'm up to and send their compliments. I've received several offers too. The highest offer I've received from a serious bidder was about $30,000.

But above all that, I make contact with lots of great people who I can offer advice on how to start their own businesses.

58. If appropriate, start selling your products on auction sites like eBay. It's easy and quickly done. Get an account today and you can begin selling immediately.

59. If you have a business selling services, make your website come alive by offering one hour of free consultation to the first person that sends you an email every Monday morning at 9 o'clock. This can be the best way to see what your visitors are wondering about – and it's definitely a great way to gather up useful.

If nobody takes you up on the offer it doesn't matter. It still shows people they have come to a generous company.

60. Buy contact details for potential customers. It depends of course on which business you're in, but you can for example get lists of details from special-interest organisations, address companies, company unions and representative associations. The smartest way is to turn to some kind of fellowship or association and buy lists from them. If that doesn't work then maybe you can join the organisation yourself and receive the official membership list with your membership materials.

Once you have the lists you have no excuse to not start up a newsletter. Make sure you get your hands on a list right away.

61. Call local companies and tell them that you would be willing to print up discount cards for their staff to use on your products. The cards would carry their company logo. Most companies will welcome your initiative to give their employees better prices and you will get customers that come back again and again to use their discount. Everyone wins (except your competitors).

62. Use gift certificates. It's easy to think that this only works for department stores, beauty salons or bookstores but that's not true. To me it seems incredibly strange that not every business offers these vouchers.

Go through all of your products and think about what could be given as gifts. It can be anything – free cleaning, a cup of coffee every morning for a month or anything else you can think of. If your products don't work as gifts, ask yourself this question: How can I make my products work as gifts?

63. If you have a physical store, you're missing out on a big benefit if you don't have a "Take one for free" box. For example, if you run a computer store and you have a box of leaflets with "Ten smart tips before you buy a new computer" you will show your customers your expertise. You show that you're not scared to answer any questions that come up and customers will come to trust you.

64. Create a *bounceback* to send with all your deliveries. A bounceback is exactly what it implies; something that bounces back quickly. Let's say that you send out a product on Monday.

You send those deliveries off with an offer on another item that complements the first. The offer lasts for a period of a few days.

65. Look more closely at all the advertisements you have seen today – do any of the companies behind the adverts need the services of your business to help them with something? Companies that send advertisements are generally hungry and want things to happen.

66. Is there someone who is considered an expert in your line of work? Send an email to him/her and ask if you can do a short interview to put up on your website. It really pays off to be associated with well-known experts.

67. If you sell services, invent a name for your services tailored to who you think would be most interested in them. You can call the packages: "The small business package", "The challengers package" or "For those who mean business". This has an entirely different feel for customers. Of course, it's important that the names really hit the mark with the customers and not just with you.

68. Buy something from your top competitor right now. Look for any flaws but also study everything they do well and strengthen these areas in your own business.

69. Start a customer of the month-page where you give a short presentation on one of your best customers. This is good for the customer as they get attention and it is good for you as you can show the world that someone really likes you and your business. Simply send an email to the customer you choose that goes something like this:

"You have been chosen as our customer of the month because... [the reason why] and we would love to ask you a few questions that will be presented on our website:

- What do you do?
- How does one best get in touch with you?
- Why did you choose to use our product/service?**"**

---

70. Send a message to your suppliers and ask them to help you with ideas for marketing your company. You are a part of their livelihood. It is in their interest that your business thrives.

71. Offers. You must have a standing offer that only applies "right now" in your web shop. Vary this and make sure that it is really only valid right now, this day or this week.

72. Add a better signature to your emails. Most people use signatures as a way to not have to manually write "Kind regards," in every email message they send or to include some basic contact information. The most common signtaure will include a telephone number, street address and the address to a web shop.

But you should take your signature one step further. It can be an important marketing tool if you use it wisely.

Here are examples of what else a signature can contain other than just contact information:

- A direct link to useful tips on your website.

- Details about your newsletter.

- Telling people about an ongoing campaign.

- Letting people know about something they can get for free.

- Short information on your most important customer perks.

- News on sales and special offers.

- News on special happenings that are coming soon.

- Let people know that they can get more information about something at your site.

- Tell people about an exciting contest.

- Other reasons for why you think people should visit your website.

73. Email the five most recent customers to have ordered something from you and ask how the process was from their perspective. Was it easy to order? What could have made it easier? Act on the answers. Do this every day so customers understand that your company cares about the customer experience.

74. Take five minutes for every potential customer that never became a customer. Which orders have you not gotten this last month? Call the ones who said no and ask them why. Was it the price, the service, the product? What did they choose instead of your product and why? Once you find out their reasons, thank them and end the conversation. In the future your salespeople should call up those who you've given quotes to but haven't as yet gotten any orders from. They should ask why the potential customers decided to go with another supplier.

Take a moment to consider whether there is anything you can do about the reasons you didn't get these sales. If something is easily fixed then send a letter to the customer and tell them that you will be better prepared next time and that you look forward to speaking with them again in the future.

From this you can get valuable information about what might have gone wrong and what you can do better than the competition.

75. If customers call to receive information about your products, make sure that you have the information ready to tell them or send to them. This will ensure that regardless of how busy you are you will be able to respond quickly.

76. Send an email to some of your best customers and tell them about a competition you are running where you ask them to take pictures of themselves using your products or services. Attract them with prizes or incentives and then use the pictures as support for your site. Take a digital camera with you when you visit customers.

77. Visit internet forums that discuss specific problems found in your line of work. Many of the questions people are asking will be similar. Draw up some answers to these questions and place these on your website. You can then direct people with queries such as these to the answers on your site (e.g. using Twitter).

78. Give customers the ability to increase the warranty time on your products for a certain price if this suits your products. If your product has a one-year warranty then offer the customer the option to pay for an additional year along with their purchase. Many of them will do this.

79. Which five websites within your niche should be linked with yours? Write this to their owners:

"Dear XYZ,

"My name is ABC and I am writing to you from [your business name]. I feel that my customers would benefit from visiting your site and believe that your customers would have an interest in my site as well. Would you like to link our sites in order to improve customer traffic for both of us?

"Regards, ABC**"**

Part 2

Generate A New Order

80. Send customers a special offer on the one-year anniversary of when they first bought something from you.

81. To whom did you ship something yesterday? Call them and ask if everything worked well in the order process from their point of view. Keep in the back of your mind the different needs they might have, or things they may want to complete their order with, and then suggest that they buy it from you.

82. Next time the flow of customers has slowed, send out an email message to your contacts. Write:

> "Call [your business name] today.
>
> "We have something special for you to say thank you for being a good customer."

This method works surprisingly well and customers will call you simply because your message makes it sound like it's very urgent to do so – they don't want to miss their chance. But be careful here. You will easily lose credibility if your offer isn't truly worth the effort. A 10% discount on something isn't going to cut it.

83. When you talk to your next customer, suggestive sell. What is the most logical extra purchase for the customer? Would you like some paper for your printer? Would you like an attachment for X? McDonalds has profited greatly by suggestive selling. Suggestive sell yourself and make sure that your salespeople do as well.

84. Try a new price on your most attractive product today and tomorrow (or for a period of a week). Today, pull the price down by 15% and tomorrow, raise it 15%. Then the next day check the number of visitors that read about the product on your website on each day as well as the sales for each day. Did you sell more when you lowered the price? Did it sell just as quickly with the higher price?

85. Who bought something from you yesterday? Send a handwritten invitation to those customers to thank them for their order and explain to them that the letter they have in their hand gives them a discount of x% on their next purchase if they order within a week/a month.

86. Let the answering machine do the work for you today! You can leave a message to say that you're sorry that you cannot pick up the phone in person and as a compensation for the callers' trouble they will receive a present with their next purchase if they state the correct code word, such as "Telephone-offer," or something similar.

That extra little present may be the incentive a customer needs to buy something from you.

87. Try to come up with a special offer that you can give to your best customers. Perhaps you have a few containers remaining of a product that is attractive but has been replaced by a new offering? If you sell ads and have a vacant spot left, it can be highly appreciated by clients to receive a good offer on this, and so on and so forth. If you provide a service that the customers might not be aware of, inform them of it.

Another idea is to offer your knowledge as a bonus product. You can give away 15 to 30 minutes of your time as an extra bonus for those who spend a certain sum of money in a day or week.

88. Hold a super-short pep rally with your salespeople first thing in the morning. What will you try to accomplish today? Make that a part of your new routine starting now. Start the next day with a follow-up on the previous day's issues. If any problems popped up – what are the solutions? If any new opportunities were revealed – how should they be handled?

89. Do you have free shipping over a certain sum? Make sure that your web developer sets this feature up for you. For example, if your minimum sum to qualify for free shipping is £50 then when a customer orders something for £23, they should see a note on their screen that says:

> **"**Your order needs £27 more to get free shipping.**"**

90. Take five minutes every day to practice selling your products on the phone so that you feel absolutely comfortable with it. Many people find it intimidating. Phone strangers and try to sell to them. Write down how it went and what you can do to improve for the next day's practice.

91. Send something interesting to your email list. It should be helpful information – a way to show that you care about them. If you only contact customers when you want to sell them something, you won't be someone people will remember. You can send them anything that will make them happy. It can be a letter to say "thanks for being a customer" or tell them about something that thrills them.

92. Pick up the phone and call several of your customers to find out what's going on in their business or lives and to see if there may be something you could help them with. You can also ask if there is something special they would really like your help with. End the conversation with: "I have sent you something fun by post." Once the conversation is over you of course have to now send them something exciting, like maybe a voucher or something else that will brighten their day a little.

93. Pick up the phone and call an old customer to see if he or she knows someone who could possibly need what you are selling.

94. Don't forget the customers that haven't bought anything from you for a while. They can become your new customers again. Contact them with a "Welcome back" offer right now.

95. If you sell something that your customers consume and will need more of, try offering the customer a subscription on your products for a better price.

96. Send your best newsletter to customers you really want and tell them that it's a good example of your newsletter and that they can sign up to it if they wish. Hopefully they will be truly interested in signing up. If they do sign up, you now have the chance to influence them every time you send out a newsletter.

97. If you force people to sign up before they buy something, get rid of that immediately. Of course you want their contact information, but perhaps the customer only wants to buy something from you this once and would like to control when and how you receive their contact information. Above all, they want to make their purchase without feeling stressed about the data you want from them before they have even made their decision. To force people to use a password in an internet shop they only visit every once in a while is a sure way to not sell very much.

98. People have different habits and customers should be able to order at any time that might suit their habits, not just during office hours.

Set up a sales phone line that can take messages throughout the day and night on an answering machine. Many phone companies have a service that provides you with a phone number that only goes to an answering machine. It's cheap and you can reach customers that only surf the net at night and do not feel comfortable ordering on the internet for security reasons. If you do this, you can write "telephone orders 24/7" next to the number on your website and in brochures.

I receive between five and twenty orders per day on our automatic answering machine. That can mean tens of thousands of pounds every year in sales.

99. Improve the subject lines of your emails. Everyone receives a lot of emails every day and you want your mail to stand out. One of the ways to improve your email subject is by making it more interesting. Instead of merely sending out a newsletter with the subject "Newsletter number 32", add some of the subject matter to the title so that the reader knows a little bit of what he/she is going to get out of reading the rest of the email. Keep it short and tell the reader why he/she should read on.

100. If you call your customers to sell to them make sure you don't sound like a typical telephone salesperson. You do not want your customers to associate you and your business with generic sales.

101. Use coupons. When customers have ordered for a certain sum of money, give them a coupon that says that they will get something for free with their next purchase over a certain amount. Show the coupon to the customer in the confirmation letter. You can also send it with the order so that they will be reminded of what they're entitled to the next time they shop.

102. Offer help with installations. If it is relevant to your business and your products it's considered very professional to offer installation help as an optional add-on.

103. Which product could you sell cheaper to your regular customers right now? Let them know about the price decrease in an offer or newsletter.

104. Get more visitors to your site. Tell customers that you've hidden five images of your company logo on your website and the first one to find them all wins a prize. This will give you a chance to give all of your products extra exposure time and if you do it well, you will sell a lot more that day.

105. People always like getting a good deal. Put together a special package of popular products or services at a super low price and then send an enthusiastic email to your customer list, your subscribers and your old contacts.

106. Invite your customers to become registered dealers of your products. Those who visit your website are already interested in your products and a small part of them will be so interested that they'll want to sell the products themselves. Make sure they get their wish – through you.

107. If you sell products in bulk, create a document to put near the bottom of the box that will become visible as the item is running low. This way customers can see where to order more of it.

The note might say something like:

> "Call 0800-7777777 to order more or visit our website at [www.yourcompany.com]."

The next time you order boxes for your products you can even have this text printed on the inside of the bottom of the box.

108. From now on include a product advertisement flyer with every product you send to a customer. If you don't have such a flyer already then write a short letter that goes something like this:

> "Thanks for buying X.
>
> "Many customers who buy X buy Y as well. We have a special offer on Y all week. Order at [your contact details]."

Part 3

Practicality At The Office

109. Let's say you have ten things to do today. Ask yourself this question: What is the most important thing for me to do right now to reach my goals? Sort all of your tasks in the order that will best help you reach your goals. This is going to make all the difference for you in the coming year. People will talk about how effective you are and scratch their heads – you are the only one who knows the simple secret.

110. Analyse your time. My experience of small companies tells me that most people invest their time in the wrong things. They feel like they're working all the time but once you take a closer look at what they're doing it's often the wrong things. Generally, at least a good half of their working hours go toward things that don't bring in money.

Don't bother maintaining your website yourself if it makes you feel stressed and takes up too much time. Get a web designer as soon as you can afford one. Don't write text for advertisements if you don't have the talent for it or you even hate writing them. You are the best at something. Do more of that instead and try to find the right person for the jobs that you don't like or can't do yourself.

As soon as you can you should delegate the administrative parts of your job and commit yourself completely to selling your products and services. Don't let administration weigh you down, you shouldn't be shuffling papers instead of doing business as every minute is valuable.

111. Take five minutes to come up with ways to make it easier for the salespeople to sell. Is there a bonus that they can give people for free once they spend more than a certain sum of money?

112. If a customer comes to you, what does he find? Are things clean and looking good? Are you sending them the message that everything is organised and under control? Take five minutes looking for things to criticise about your company's image that any customer might also find.

113. Look over your information material. Make a note to yourself that in the next brochure you will have concrete offers, not just information.

114. Look at your merchandise – which ones can you make a more complete package of and then sell at a package price? Find out and get to it! Test your package on the internet. Keep adjusting the products in the package along with price until you find the winning combination.

115. Send an email to your staff right away and get them to tell you what customers generally ask for that you do not already provide. Act on what you learn.

116. Are you spoiled with being able to easily define who your best customers are? Is it, for example, women from 40 to 50 years of age, who live in the suburbs and have a career? Write it up on a large note and put it on your wall. Your subconscious will be working on how to reach this target group in the future. Your best customer group represents solid income for your company and you should always be thinking of different, smart things to offer them.

117. Take five minutes to split up your marketing tasks into categories of "good idea to do" and "must do" every day. In other words, always ask yourself the question: "Is this really necessary to do?" before every single task that is before you.

118. Praise several of your salespeople every single day and you will see what happens to their work performance. It's not a difficult thing to measure. Go and find someone to say something kind to right away.

119. If you have salespeople, take a £50 note and hang it up on a wall – the person who sells the most that day gets to take it home. If that idea doesn't work find some other way to give them a direct reward now and then.

120. Set up a special wall, folder or some kind of bulletin board to present your competitors' advertisements, brochures and other marketing materials. Make sure that all of your employees read and understand what the competition is doing. You can organise your competitors' activities into different groups, for example: price pressures, quality, customer service, and so on.

121. Prepare for tomorrow today. At the end of every work day take an empty piece of paper and write down everything you want to do the next day and in which order it should be done. The next day you can get right to it. You will feel an incredible peace as you tick item after item off your "to do" list.

A rule I've used for the last ten years is that every day I do five things that bring me closer to my goal. So over that period I've done 18,250 things that have taken me closer to my goal! You can do the same thing. It only takes one normal work week to do 25 things.

122. Always assume that the customers who request price quotes from you most likely ask other companies as well. What can you do to improve your quotes? And how can you send them out faster? Many companies sit on an request for well over a week before finally getting them out. Inform all of your salespeople to send out price quotes quicker.

123. Find a glass jar and place a pen and two different coloured notebooks next to it. Everything you can think of that will improve your business should from now on be written down on a note and placed in the jar. Allocate one colour of note to mean "Important" and the other colour should be for "If there is time." When you have time on your hands, take one of the notes out of the jar.

124. Take out your business card. Does your card entice you to check out your website? Why not? Throw out your business card and make a new one with text on the back as well. The idea behind this is to use the back in some way to help your customers. It could be tips on how to take care of flowers or references to good content on your website... whatever is relevant to your business. You can also use the back of your business card as a special voucher for the next purchase.

125. If you don't want to throw out your old business cards take one from your drawer and write on it: "The next time I print cards I need to do something smart with the back of them."

126. Have a short meeting with your salespeople. They should try asking customers throughout the day if they know someone else that would appreciate what they're selling – this way you can get their addresses or phone numbers and when you call them you can refer to your old customer in the conversation:

> **"**XX thought you would be interested in...**"**

127. Have you just come back from a promising meeting with clients or potential clients? Put five minutes into writing an enthusiastic note to the people in the meeting about how you perceived the contents of the meeting and that you're anxious to get started on everything that was talked about. Very few companies do this. Your customers will like to see that you're eager to start on the job.

128. Have you marketed your internet store in your physical store? There are so many things to do in a store to draw traffic to your website. Special vouchers for use on internet orders are one thing, recommended tips in the field of your business is another.

129. Place a sign on your phone – and the phones of everyone in the company – with the word "SMILE" on it. People do actually hear it when the person they are talking to on the phone is smiling.

130. Fix those gaping holes in your activity. All companies have areas that they can get better in and now is the time to take care of them, to plug the leaks. It can be bad routines, for example if you miss following up on all the offers you send out. It can be that you promised yourself to always call the customers after delivery to make sure that everything worked out but you haven't kept up with that. It's time to make all those things you'd want other people to recognise that your business stands for into a solid routine that everyone in your company follows.

131. How do you reward yourself and your employees for delivering perfect service? We are all only human. It doesn't matter if you as a boss think that your employees are already paid quite enough to give perfect service; they will give even better service if you notice and reward them when they do well. Your own reward will soon enough show up in the business's performance.

132. Try answering "yes" to everything for a day. Challenge yourself to always say yes to anything the customer asks for. It works almost every single time. If the customer wants money off say yes – if they buy two.

133. Instruct your salespeople to always ask customers how they heard about your company. Ask them to write it down so that you can figure out what things make customers come to you. If the references come from an unpaid source, reward those who've recommended you.

Draw up a standard letter where you only need to sign your name and send it along with a fun little item to the person who sent the customer your way. Tell them it's your policy to always reward those who refer customers to you – this should make them keen to recommend more people to you in the future.

134. Make a daily game out of getting customer references and see how many times per day you can ask customers if they know any people or businesses that might be interested in what you have to offer. Include your salespeople in the game, they will end up with a much easier job and can earn more money with this simple contest. If a customer has taken advantage of a special offer then this is easy – you need only thank the customer for the order and then ask if he/she knows anyone who would also benefit from the same offer.

135. Create a "Two things rule." The two things rule means that you focus on the two very most important things to do today and do them well.

136. Limit your starting time in the morning to three five-minute periods. Take five minutes to get your coffee and talk to others, five minutes to read emails and five minutes to check the news. You can get an enormous advantage here as most people, according to research, aren't able to really get going with their work for at least the first hour of the day. That's 45 minutes of time saved that you can spend on calling customers, which is almost three hours a week and within a month will become an entire day of work – just by getting started quicker.

I know what you're thinking; you're not a machine. But it is better to give yourself a specified amount of time to sit around catching up with your colleagues without needing to have a bad conscience about it the entire time.

137. Buy post-it notes in different colours, for example, yellow and blue. The yellow notes will be used as your "today notes" where you write down everything you want to complete today and the blue will be for your long-term projects. When you go home, there shouldn't be a single yellow note laying around your work place. If anything there might be a couple stuck to your computer screen telling you what you need to be doing tomorrow.

138. When you first arrive at work, sit down comfortably, close your eyes and envision how the day will unfold and what should be completed before you go home. Aim, perhaps, to reach three goals today. This can feel a little strange, but it works for many people. Try it out, it only takes about 10 to 20 seconds. If you don't collect yourself in the morning in this way then the chances are that you will work without a clear aim and fail to achieve what you want to.

139. Take a five-minute break every hour during the day. Walk around the office, surf your favourite website, throw a ball up and down. To know in this way that the "school bell will ring soon" is going to make it easier and more fun for you to work harder.

140. Take five minutes every day to worry. There are several psychologists who claim that people worry a lot less in general if they have a specific time in the day to worry about things. During this time you could be worrying about possible roadblocks your competitors might throw in your way, or about what customers think of you. Worry about your company's survival and write down your concerns; but without taking more than five minutes to do so. That's enough.

The next day look over your notes and you will probably notice that maybe it wasn't as bad as you imagined, or you might have come up with a few solutions to the problems you were worrying about.

Practice disconnecting things that aren't so relevant just right now. Ask yourself the question: "Can I do something about this problem right now?" If the answer is no, don't throw away your time on it – spend your energy on something else. It may not be all that easy all the time, but for me it helps tremendously to ask myself that one question. It gets rid of some of the problems in any case.

141. Add a blank row to your invoices. In this space write about the current week's offer on your website. Make sure that the week's offer is always at the same address, with different offers every week.

142. It helps to prioritise your tasks each day. Everyone who sells things should always make whatever is "closest to cash" their number one priority every day. This might be to call a possible customer, write an amazing offer or sales letter, or to close a business deal. Write a big note and put it on the wall: "What is closest to cash?"

143. Make an idea box and explain to staff that from now on, all ideas that lead to finding customers, keeping old customers, or to marketing the business better will be rewarded.

144. Write down your goal for your website this year. What should it accomplish? Is the target to make a certain amount of money that you can clearly verify came from the website? Should it draw a certain number of subscribers to your newsletter or encourage a certain number of people to contact you in some way such that you can verify they come via your site? Write the goal down and place it somewhere you will always see it.

145. Buy a notepad or journal. Use this as a place for people to register their interest in your newsletter when you meet them out and about, as opposed to when they are looking at your website. You can take this with you when you go to off-site business meetings.

146. Many people are stuck in the "Facebook swamp", meaning that they hop on to Facebook whenever they're bored and aren't sure what to do. If you can avoid these kinds of time traps you will actually have a competitive edge right there.

147. Take a look at your bookkeeping – which of your products sells out fastest? It's strange but most companies can agree with the 80-20 rule, which means that 80% of the revenue comes from about 20% of the products. What can you do to generate more income from the 20% of top products, and what can you do to earn more from the 80% of less lucrative products?

Your best-selling products can often become products that you don't care much about because they sort of slip your mind and you don't worry about them, but that's wrong. You should think about how you can further expose those products. Consider that if many people have wanted that product, there are sure to be many more people still out there who will also want it. Give your best sellers more space.

148. Make sure there is unique content on your website that isn't easy to come by. If you sell carpets you could give a guide on how people can tell the difference between a handmade carpet and one that was mass produced. If you're an expert on leadership then you should give a clear guide on how to be a better boss. .

149. Do you have connections to people who can do jobs that you can't find the time for? If you don't already have a web designer it's time you got one, because in all likelihood you don't have the time to sit down and do everything on your website that you want done. Ask someone who owns a site that you like which web designer created it.

150. Write a short but meaningful note on a customer's invoice:

> **"**We are glad that you chose us.**"**

Include a chocolate bar or another small present to make them all the happier.

151. Find an empty wall in your office. Write: "About us in the press" on a large note and stick it on the wall. This will remind you to hunt for publicity you have received to add to the wall and to come up with things that journalists can write about you and your company.

152. Which one of your employees really ought to get a new and exciting task that can boost their motivation? Give them that task as soon as possible!

153. Set a goal for tomorrow before you go home today. This can be easier said than done if you don't really make up your mind to do it. Write on a note what tomorrow's goals are, what you at the very least need to get done. Put the list on your keyboard so that it will be the first thing you see in the morning.

154. Explain to your employees and to yourself that you now have a new email policy. Every email will be answered within five minutes/one hour/two hours/three hours. The closer you get to five minutes, the more products you will sell.

155. Tell your employees to follow up better. If a customer asks about a product, follow up within a day to ask if they were satisfied with the answer they received or if they need to know more. This is a good way to show the customers that you care about them.

156. Every now and again you get a chance to present your company to a group of people. Panic! Relax – here's a method for writing a speech in only five minutes. Sit down in a corner with a piece of paper and a pen and just follow the points below.

- Decide what message you want to give to your listeners. Do you want to congratulate them for all the good they have done, give them advice or sell a new idea to them?

- Start with a rough draft. Write these topics first: Main message, Opening statement, Support points, and Ending.

- Write down your main message in one single sentence in plain English, for example, "For a company to survive in the future they must double their sales." You write this first since everything else you say from here on should support this message.

- Think about your main message and write down your ending next. The ending could be to encourage people to act in some way. You will tell your listeners what they should do once you've finished speaking (buy a product from you, smile more often at their customers, come up to speak with you and get your contact information, etc). The best way to write an ending is to do it according to this model: If you want to have... (the desired result)... then it's time for you to... (what they should be doing to achieve it).

- Now that you know what point you want to make and how to wrap it up, it's time to look at your support points. Come up with five different points that support your message. As soon as you have five, choose the best three and throw in some statistics or a personal story that can support each point if you can. Your audience wants to be entertained so if you have an amusing story that supports what you want to say share it with them. It makes it easier for your audience to relate.

■ And last – work on the opening. Come up with a few catchy phrases to really hook your audience and keep them on their toes. It could be a challenge, a question, some cold hard facts, a thought-provoking quote, or a story.

After that, just take a deep breath, gather some courage, smile and step forward.

157. Set goals that interest you. Answer the questions below, perhaps saying your responses out loud to yourself after every question. The aim with this is that you actually formulate what you want, where you are going and why you actually bother getting out of bed every morning.

1. What do you want?

Here you will formulate exactly what you want (do not confuse it with what you don't want), that you can accomplish yourself (not what you want someone else to arrange for you). Try to be as specific as possible. "I want more money" is not specific. "I want to earn £10,000 more every month" is specific.

2. What would it mean if you got what you want?

The answer to this question will explain what your efforts will give you.

3. How will you know when you've got it?

Describe what you will see, hear and feel when you get it.

4. How will you and everybody else know when you have got it?

Describe what others will see, hear and feel when you get it.

5. When do you want it?

Describe when you expect to get there.

6. What is it that stops you from already having it?

This helps you see what types of obstacles lie in your path. Once you see that, it will be a lot easier to know what to do to overcome them.

7. How will the things you want affect other parts of your life?

This is something that can be easy to forget. There are probably going to be both positive and negative consequences to consider.

8. What have you done today to help you reach this goal?

Take a closer look at what resources and tools you have that will help you get there.

9. What do you need to get first in order to reach your goal (knowledge or something else)?

It's time to get specific again. A positive attitude is always good to have, but it's better to say "I'm going to take a course in telephone sales and get so good at it that I'll love doing it, instead of like now, when I get tongue tied whenever customers don't want to buy anything."

10. What is the easiest way to get to your goal?

What is the absolute first step towards your goal? What can you do right now, within five minutes, to get one step closer? Are there many ways to start? Which one is likely the best? Which way is the fastest and is it possible there will be a conflict between speed and quality?

Life in sales: lift yourself in five minutes

Imagine that you've been working hard for a while and none of the names on your list want to buy anything from you. You've fallen into a slump. For every "no" you get, your self-confidence only sinks lower and you're being assaulted with feelings of hopelessness – welcome to the everyday world of sales.

None of this is as bad as you might think. Yes, it's lonely, tough and hopeless sometimes. You have to take control of it, before it takes control of you.

Talk to yourself instead of letting your lack of confidence dictate to you. Take a deep breath and say to yourself: "One day sooner or later, I'm going to become very successful at this." If you have a mentor or someone to talk to – do it. Get rid of the weight that your lack of self-confidence tries to place on your shoulders. If you are part of a network, talk it over with them. If it is easy to succeed, then why isn't everybody successful? And why do all the people who have become successful tend to talk about the times when they felt like the biggest failure, as if it was something they're glad they went through? Because it was worth it.

Stop caring about things that happened in the past and start caring about what is happening right now. You've heard it before but sometimes you need to hear it again. You can't change what happened in the past. The only thing you need to concern yourself with is how to avoid repeating the same mistakes. Try new approaches!

Try to visualise yourself being successful and make your goals clear to yourself. Is it a Porsche, a new house, a trip around the world every year or a growing and healthy business? Don't be shy. Someone who works in sales does what many people are too scared to do; to be faced with hearing the word NO. If you are that brave, you need to know what you'll get for it. You deserve to reach your goals.

If nothing else helps then bring out this list:

- It's OK to feel a bit low sometimes. You're not a robot.
- You have a hard job – but it's also very rewarding when you do hit the mark.
- Don't forget that a salesperson's job is to take the lead and boldly cut a path for all the others behind them to follow – cool job!
- Don't forget that you're the one that pushes the company forward. You mean something.
- It's hard to sell, it can be a thankless job, but whenever you help a client really take off and get to hear their gratitude, it's worth all the pain.
- You are a salesperson because... (this is where you fill out why you go to your job every day).
- Put on your favourite music, preferably in your car, take a drive and sing along.

Do you see where I'm coming from? It's OK to feel down sometimes. Don't fall for the cheesy stereotype with salespeople who walk around looking like they swallowed a sunrise – in my 20 years in the business I've seen them all and unfortunately also witnessed many of them fall.

It's OK to feel like it's rough sometimes. It's even good and healthy for sales. Don't ever forget that.

Part 4

90 Questions That Can Really Speed Up Your Sales!

I suggest that the following questions should be placed in a container as notes which you will draw once a day. The instructions are:

1. Buy two containers.

2. Cut out all of the questions from the book and fold them up. Put them in container 1.

3. Draw a note every day, answer the question on the note, and do something about it!

4. Place your "done" question in the second container.

Keep doing this until your first container is empty. Then, go to your second container which is now full of notes and start the process over again. This way you're getting several important questions asked about your business each day, and every question will help your company to progress.

If you are reading this as an eBook, why not pick a question at random every day, answer it and take the action needed.

The point of this process is not to kill yourself trying to do everything all at once. The point is that the marketing of your business should improve just a little bit each and every day you're at work.

With these questions you will either take the time to deal with them one at a time, meaning you can come up with an answer that fits you instantly, or you will automatically take the most important questions to heart and ponder them for a while. In whichever way the answers come to you, I guarantee that they will strengthen your business.

Under each of the questions are some empty lines – write down some spontaneous answers in this space for you to think about in more detail later.

Five-minute questions to ask yourself

158. Can you merge your business with another to have a stronger position in the market? Which business would that be?

You probably know the answer right away. The business you're looking for will make your own business stronger; therefore you should be looking among businesses that can complete your own in different ways. It could also be a competitor that you can buy up, or work together with. If for example you are more focused on quality and the competition focuses on volume, you could help sell each other's products.

----

159. Have you thought about joint advertising with other businesses on your street? Together you can cover the local area. You can also help each other out through recommending each other, keeping coupons in each other's stores, composing ads together, etc. What can you do today to strengthen your business relationships with your neighbours? What suggestions could you go over to your neighbour and tell them about right now?

----

160. Can you give a customer's first purchase away for free? How would that work in your line of business? To give away the first one for free is a sure fire way to draw in new customers and show them what you're all about.

A consultant can give their first half hour away for free. Beauty product salespeople can give away a sample. Let's pretend that you, according to law, were obligated to give away something for free in order to gain customers. What would you give away and how would you do it? Do you dare trying this?

----

161. Can you start a class in a field that you specialise in? This is a good way to attract new customers. One suggestion on how to do this is to talk to your closest business organisation. Contact them with a suggestion right away.

----

162. Would you, truthfully, like to be a customer of your own business? If yes, congratulations! If not, what would have to be different for you to change your mind?

----

163. How could you make your product a little more luxurious? Think about this for five minutes. Maybe there is a business that gives out a free product that you could slip into your own package when you send a product out. Maybe you could devise an information product that completes what you sell. You have the knowledge of your field – why not use that to create a higher value in what you sell.

----

164. If you sell services, how could you use your website to tell people how to order the coaching and personnel management package which includes X for the price of Y. Many people who are afraid that things will become too expensive will be more inclined to trust you if you state a set price. When you later meet with the customer you may find out that their needs were in fact greater – or even smaller – than what was first assumed.

----

165. Think about: How can you give your customers an offer they can't refuse? What reasons can you give your visitors to choose your business over the competition?

----

166. Ask yourself: If I had a million to invest in marketing this company, what would I spend it on? Which section of the business, or which products or services, would I spend the money on? The products or services that you have identified here as the ones you have the most faith in are the ones where you should also invest most of your time.

----

167. Which one of your sales channels is the best right now? This is a question you should be able to answer right away if you're a good marketer. If you know which channels work the best, you also know which ones aren't working as well as you would like them to.

Now you have two options – either further develop the ones that work the best (that's what I would do) or take care of the worst. In other words – pour your resources into that which you already know to work and put the things that are not working on the back burner. That is unless you see undeveloped potential in the ones that aren't working and decide to expand there instead.

In any case, you need to make a decision about where you're going to put your energy right now – and what you will put on the back burner for the time being. Note down which channels are best and what you can do to develop them even further.

----

168. Write a short sales letter to your best friend on whatever it is that you're selling. This practice helps you to get rid of the BS, and stick to the things that your friend would respect and appreciate. Then, transfer the same text to a letter to your actual customers, because your customers truly are your company's best friends.

----

169. If you had a whole stack of money to invest in some special part of your business to make the biggest possible change for the positive, what would you put it towards? Do you understand what an interesting angle this is? You may perhaps need to uproot and weed out something that's just draining your business. It's difficult to do, but feels great when it's done! What would you invest more in? What would you stop putting time, effort and money into if you could? Act on what you come up with.

----

170. To be the market leader of your area of business in ten years' time, where should you put your time and company resources to get there? Shrug off any boundaries, real or perceived – write down exactly what you would need to have and what you would need to do in order to become the leader of your market. Don't be shy.

When you've written it all down and perhaps realise that your current resources aren't enough, think over how you can either obtain them, or how you can get closer to your goal even with less than optimal resources.

- This is what it takes to be the leader of the market.

_____

_____

- These are the resources that I have today.

_____

_____

- This is how I can take the first steps.

_____

_____

171. What would make your customers completely overjoyed? Can you make it happen today? Your job is now to come up with five things you can do to make this happen quickly and cost effectively.

_____

_____

_____

172. Is it time to do what so many others have done – skip the retailers and start selling directly to the end customer? Do you sell your products and services online yet? The internet has given many small business owners a chance to rise in a hundred different ways, but the best thing is that they no longer have to bow down to larger franchises and can turn directly to the customer with the help of a good website.

My own book publishing company is a great example of this. More than 95% of the books that we sell are shipped directly from us to the end customer. This makes it both faster for the customer and far more profitable for us. Throw away all preconceived notions that "people just don't do it this way in our line of work!" Instead, think like this: if the internet was the only sales channel you were allowed to use, how would you best sell your products there?

You can find a solution that is much better than the one you're using now. It doesn't matter if at the moment you only sell to dealers; you should become your own dealer online. It's stupid to not try to reach the customers directly – without a middleman. How can you get this done within two months? Think it over and make a plan. At the very least, you'll get a sales channel that complements what it is that you do outside of the internet.

---

173. Ask yourself: What can I do today to make to make my company's reputation twice as strong and positive within six months? Now we're talking about things that many businesses never have the time for (or so they say). To work with the press, to create an unbeatable, famous guarantee. To shock the customers in a positive way that the competition has not thought of yet. What could you do fairly easily to help strengthen your company's reputation, even within the next month?

----

174. Could you create your own award within your line of work? Give the winner and all the nominees a logo to put on their websites. When someone clicks on the logo they will be taken to your website. Don't believe that most awards are given for noble causes only – they are more often just another way for organisations, magazines and companies to profile themselves as the most important player in the market. You should do the same.

----

175. Think about whether your website could become a resource that reviews other products related to your own. If you do this it will be easy to get people to link to your website (especially the businesses that have been given a good review). You simply try different products and list what is good and bad about them so that your visitors will find it easier to make a well-informed choice.

----

176. Could you be a local resource in the news field? If it fits with your line of work, why not make a report on local happenings in your field of business or in the area that will attract the kind of customers you want.

----

177. People are in a hurry. They have got in touch with you because they want to buy now. If you answer them quickly you will have the best chance to stay in the game. Here are a few important questions to ponder:

- Do you and your staff know what should be sent out as a response to different types of inquiries?

- Do you have electronic versions of your responses for those who would like their replies through email or downloaded from your website?

- Do you have updated and relevant material in print for those who prefer that?

- Do you have fax versions for those who prefer information by fax?

- Are your staff well versed in the technology your company uses, so that information gets sent on its way quickly?

----

178. Do you have established routines for catching all inquiries so that they can be dealt with continuously by all concerned parties? In order to not risk certain things slipping between your fingers it's good to have some sort of database that all the relevant people in your company have easy access to (or even simply a plastic drawer labelled "Possible clients").

----

179. Do you have routines for taking care of and evaluating inquiries before sending them on to your salespeople? This of course demands a clear definition of what actually constitutes a qualified inquiry – everybody should know and understand these definitions. Your job is to come up with questions to ask possible clients to try to estimate how interesting they actually are.

----

180. Do you have a system for how particular tasks are passed to the right members of the sales team? Inquiries are worthless if they are not sent to the right salesperson for a quick follow-up. Your distribution of errands and tasks can never be fast enough, it's as simple as that.

In a perfect world, the salesperson should be notified the second after the customer has called and the sales team should also handle all inquiries as prioritised tasks.

Many business deals have rotted away on Post-it notes. Think about what the easiest way would be for your company to get the contact in touch with sales. It can be by email, telephone or even yelling through the office.

----

181. Do you have routines for nurturing customers that aren't ready to buy something this very instant? Salespeople usually focus (as they should) on customers who will buy something right now, or soon. But it is also important to understand there is a large group of people out there who will contact you when they are not quite ready to buy just yet. Good routines for dealing with customers who are obviously interested but not quite ready to make the leap could lead to lots of new closures. In these cases it's simply down to building relationships and this can be done in several ways:

- You can call them.
- You can email them.
- You can have an electronic or physical newsletter.
- You can make sure that these future customers end up on other outgoing mailing lists.

You should see these customers as important and put in place routines to help you keep in regular contact with them.

----

182. What are the ten most important things your business can help future customers with? Schedule some time to mention them on your website.

----

183. Look at your website and think about how you are going to start cross selling – if you don't already do this. Customers like getting recommendations on other products or services that fit with what they have in their basket already.

What can you offer your customers as additional services? This may include gift-wrapping, selling batteries for products that need them, and so on. What can you easily add to your product that you can charge extra for? Those who want to buy a flashlight probably need batteries as well. Those who buy a tent might be interested in sleeping bags and ground mats. Perhaps there are even things you can add without charging more and without any trouble on your part, but which will still be seen as a valuable addition by customers?

Make it easy for your customers to find closcly-related products and you will sell a lot more. Schedule time to putting in a system that shows closely-related items to whatever the customer is already buying. If you have a web designer, email them and tell them that you want a system that does just that.

----

184. What could you create that would benefit your old customers? Can you compensate them in some way, give them something special or maybe even start a customer club just for them? It doesn't matter if you have five or 5000 customers – everybody likes preferential treatment.

----

185. What works particularly well right now and how can you make sure it stays that way? This point is about reflection. Don't start waving your axe around just because you have one. Don't start fixing things that aren't broken.

----

186. How quickly and how well does your business adapt to changes in your customers' lives, the demands of the market, technical development, staff needs and economic issues? We live in a time where everything changes so fast that you can barely keep up. Take control and try to stay ahead of the game as much as possible.

What instruments can you start using to help you keep up? It can be as simple as subscribing to an important magazine, holding a development meeting once a month, or subscribing to a competitor's newsletter.

What is the best and most practical way for you to keep moving ahead?

----

187. Who are the five most important people in the company and what can you do for them to make sure they want to stick around for a long time?

----

188. Which systems and processes work so well that you take them for granted? What can be done to improve them?

----

189. What does your business have that is really fantastic but that hasn't quite reached the market in the way you would want it to?

----

190. What are the major highlights of your products today and what are you doing now and tomorrow to come up with the next big thing? Here, I am of course thinking about product and service development. All marketers must stay ahead of the market and know exactly what to do to avoid falling behind.

So what's the big deal about your product/service today and what should it be tomorrow? Write down three things straight from the heart that will give the things you sell a competitive edge for the future.

----

191. Should you start a club in your line of work? What would it look like? What would be the easiest way to recruit members to the club? How could this club lead to more business for you?

----

192. Which products/services could you make a flyer for to distribute where your future clients are? Would you market the product directly or perhaps create some interesting content to draw the reader to your website? Can you come up with a mini-test with multiple choice questions that will work as a magnet to draw people to your website?

----

193. Content is the heart of the internet. Who ought to be part of a group dedicated to taking care of, creating and updating the information on your website?

----

194. Whatever you sell, there may be many different agents out there that can help you sell it. Who could be a potential agent for selling your product? If you sell natural health products, don't just turn to health food stores. Make sure to find different mediums for particular products. Hair products to hair dressers, special oils for naprapathy, etc. All of your products do not need to be sold at the same locations. Make a list.

----

195. If you had to, how would you go about making your customers your salespeople? Take five minutes to think it over. What can you do to make your most satisfied customers recommend you to others and what can you give them to encourage this? Add a recommendations feature to your most important pages so that it is easy for your visitors to tell others about your site.

----

196. How can you increase the value of every order? Those who sell services should complement them with a few related products to sell to customers. Is there something that you have or could come up with that is free for you to include with every order? What would that be? Would you be able to train yourself and your staff to always try to suggestive sell this item to customers? What can you do to encourage your workers to get comfortable with this and do it with every customer?

----

197. Is there an organisation for your business sector that can gather possible customers for you? Do they have a magazine that you can write articles in? Do they, or would they like to, hold competitions? You can stand ready to help out and offer the products you sell as prizes. Which magazines/organisations will you send the following message to today?

> **"**Hello!
>
> **"**I read your website every day and I wonder if you would like to host a competition? We have an overstock of (name of product here) that you could use for prizes if you would be interested.**"**

---

198. Take five minutes to ponder ways of creating an automated reselling system.

We asked ourselves this very question at my company Redaktionen and came up with an easy way to give those interested in selling our books a free online bookstore to connect to their websites. All they do is link to their bookstore from their website – all of the administration, shipping and bills are then handled by us.

Can you do the same thing and have other people resell your products online? Are there any other ways to get resellers that you can think of?

---

199. How are you going to find ways to get your products in front of a wider audience? Your products might be appropriate for shop windows, for example. If your products do shine in this way, then many companies may want to place your products in their shop windows.

Contact companies that are not in direct competition with your own. Tell them that you would like to place your product in their windows the next time they start thinking of redecorating them with a new theme. Suggest a theme yourself. Which companies or organisations could be interested in this? Write down at least five.

----

200. Ask yourself these questions today (and if it takes more than five minutes, that's OK!):

■ Where are we today?

■ Where do we want to go?

- How do we get there?

----

201. Think over which of your future customers are just laying in wait at the moment. Think about what you can do today so that those future customers will think of you first the next time they are ready to buy.

----

202. Take five minutes to think about what would happen if your biggest client decided to leave you today. Make a plan for your business to become less vulnerable. And while you do that, also think about ways you can make sure your biggest client does not leave you. Have you taken them for granted? Have you gotten lazy in some way that you need to deal with?

----

203. If an unconditional guarantee isn't offered by your competitors at present, what would it mean for your own business if you offered one?

----

204. I have a Rolex watch, which is worth a lot to me because it was expensive. I like to have a real piece of quality craftsmanship on my wrist. It serves as an everyday reminder of what quality is and that I aspire to achieve the same within my business.

Where can you raise your prices so that you will also become known as a top-quality dealer? Maybe you can come up with three different versions of the things you sell – a cheaper product for a low budget, a standard product and a premium product at a high price for those who want to pay more.

If you were forced by law to come up with a product or service that should represent the very top of the line in terms of price, what would it be?

----

205. What's the cheapest way to draw new customers to your business? Before you invest thousands of pounds on advertising, think about whether you could profit just as much by simply calling some of your old customers.

---

206. Sit down and close your eyes for a second. Pretend that you are your own customer. What does he/she really expect from you? What would make them want it even more?

---

207. How can you create your own tradition that customers come to know and recognise? When the winter is at its worst, and people feel the most hopeless, could you offer your customers a little bit of sunshine? For example, you could send over a flowerpot with seeds for summer flowers. Feel free to come up with your own ideas!

---

208. Why don't all restaurants allow customers to sign up to a special list so that they can take part in the restaurant's future plans, special theme nights, or whatever else is happening? Can you do that in your line of work? Can you put it up on your website right now? Can you put up a poster about it in your store?

----

209. What would make your customers use more of your product each time they use it?

----

210. What would cause your customers to use your product on more occasions?

----

211. What would get your distributors to stock more of your product?

---

212. How can you convey to customers that they can have fun using your product?

---

213. How can you make your packaging more fun? Can you make it taller, thinner, smaller, transparent, or of some different material? If the packaging is of lower quality, will the customers believe that the product is, too?

---

214. Take time to consider if you should start using discounts for regular customers. You could produce a card that you sign every time the customer shops. After five times they get a little present. You of course make sure to collect their names and addresses when they get their card. How could you do this in the easiest way possible?

If you have an online store, give your regular customers a code to put in the order form or surprise them with discounts.

_____

_____

_____

215. If you sell a product where customers might benefit from specific educational information, why not throw in a "how to" video so that the customer can see step-by-step how to install that new equipment or plant those seeds in the very best way?

What would be the best way to get started with a project like this? Can you approach a local school or college and ask the students there to help? Providing customers with a "how to" video could actually be the very thing that encourages them to buy your product instead of a competitor's!

_____

_____

_____

216. Can you host a product auction? Let the customers enter their bids in your store or online. You should of course set a starting price that no one can bid under, which could even be set a bit lower than your normal purchase price.

In the United States many stores have tried this concept and noticed that the rest of their sales increase so much that they can even sell the products in the auction for less than their usual price. Make your store or website one where people can't refuse paying a visit because they know there will always be something fun taking place.

---

217. How do you measure customers' happiness? If customers come back, that can mean that they are satisfied. It can also mean that your company's telephone number is the first one they see and that the customer doesn't even think about its value because you don't have anything all that special to offer.

Think about whether you yourself would want to be a client at your business. What would be the top reasons to be, and not to be, your own customer? And don't be kidding yourself – there are always some reasons both for and against.

In my business, for example, working against us is the fact that it's hard for customers to find the time and energy to read books and try new things. Our books also aren't widely available in bookstores and it some customers may perceive it as a risk to buy a book when you cannot first flip through its pages.

-----

218. Imagine a situation where your visitors would be asked to pay for the contents of your website – what types of content would you create for this? Why not create that very content – but give it away for free!

-----

219. What (or who) is the weakest link in your company? What is it that you should have done, but didn't do? How can this be improved?

-----

220. Write down a dream sales figure – the number will be next month's sales target. Put it up on the wall in front of you so that you have something to fight for.

----

221. When will your sales staff and marketers (if you are alone, this means you) get to do something fun as a reward since they (you) work so hard? Write down what you will do on which date and send it to your sales staff.

----

222. Write down three things you can do today to make your employees feel like they are an important part of something.

----

223. Who are you jealous of in the business world? How can you become more like them?

----

224. Can you afford to open a new business in another place? It can mean a lot just to be in the right geographical location for many products and services.

----

225. Can you make your business a franchise where other people could get the rights to sell your products in their own market?

----

226. Do you have administrative personnel who are paid a fixed salary? Think up a way to make them more motivated and then see if more customers trickle in.

----

227. What kind of a super prize can you have in order to encourage everyone to come to your site and partake in a competition this month? If you have a business that customers visit, what kind of super prize can you give that will motivate all those who come to you to compete for by answering a simple question and giving you their names and addresses?

----

228. If it's easy for you to create some sort of entertainment on your site, do it. It could be informative blog posts, quizzes, games or funny pictures that will give your website more appeal.

----

229. I am always astonished that there are no emergency response costs at most service companies. It's just incredible to me that hardly any of them use that kind of pricing. You might call a handyman who says they can help fix your bathroom for £35 an hour but they're not going to be free for six weeks. Why don't they add that they could start tomorrow if you'd be willing to pay £60 per hour? I don't understand it.

Could you utilise emergency costs in your business somehow? How would that work for you? Imagine if you were somehow forced to do this. Pretend that it's illegal not to and see if you come up with any ideas.

-----

230. Take a moment to consider what you can give away for free to your customers that they can pass on to their friends. A voucher? A calendar? What are you sending to your customers today where you could also include something for them to give away to other potential customers?

-----

231. Find yourself. Sit down and think. Turn off everything that could disturb you and think about how you could best increase your sales. Is it by finding a partner? Is it with strengthening your service? Is it through finding other distribution channels? What would you like to try your hand at that you believe could give a big boost to your business?

-----

232. When you meet up with your clients what kind of present could you give them – or what could they receive from you when they leave? Don't ever let a client leave your office or store empty handed. To give them an actual product is best, but it could also be a special offer for next week, a brochure, a gift or a flyer. It can also just be a simple piece of paper with an advertisement that shows exactly what great resources you have.

What would be most suitable for you to give to your customers? What would they appreciate getting? What would get them to go home and look up your website?

Part 5

45 Super-smart Things To Do As Soon As You Can

If you are like me there are probably things you have to do that you really don't feel like doing, or you simply forget that it's a good idea to do them. To get these things done it's useful to plan a specific time for them. This part of the book is about things that you never quite find the time to do and so therefore you need to schedule time for.

My tip is to take a few minutes to note down those things below that have to fit into your schedule so that you are forced to do them – you make your calendar, quite frankly, boss. Perfect for those of us that are a bit lazy by nature but still know that it is important to move forward.

In order to make full use of this chapter you will need your calendar/smartphone or whatever it is that you use to plan your time to hand. And you have to promise yourself that you will do whatever you've written down, whenever the day it is allocated to comes around.

Note: Some of the paragraphs in this chapter are pretty long so don't waste time trying to write the whole text down. My advice would be to write "Do point 251 from *The 5-Minute Marketer*" in your calendar.

233. Schedule two hours to see how much money your latest advertisements and marketing expenditure brought in. What really happened between the two dates when the advertisement was run? Call the sales department, count how many orders you got during those days, or check the traffic on your website at that time. Simply, was the ad worth the cost? Has the money you spent on marketing been worth it?

234. Make the most-visited pages on your website easier for people to scan quickly. If your current page consists of large blocks of text it's usually a good idea to throw in a little extra breathing space between paragraphs. This way it will be easier for people to read and take in.

235. Immediately establish a plan that makes you ready for any changes that touch on your business' most sensitive points – the things you know are your weaknesses. This plan makes you feel prepared; you will know what to do, which creates the incentive to act. For example, if someone releases a new product that your dealers like better than yours, if your suppliers raise their prices or change things around, what will you do?

236. Is your domain name easy to remember? If not, then get a domain that's easy to remember and easy to market. I am bemused every time I see an advertisement on TV with a complicated domain name that people will forget as soon as the programme they were watching comes on again.

In addition, think about what other domains you could have pointing to your main website. If a company is called Perfect Piping System and has the address www.perfectpiping.com and manufactures a system to clean sewage that everyone should have at home, why do they not register www.cleanyourpipes.com as well and point it to their main website.

If you're advertising in any form, you have to make it easy for anyone who's interested to take part in your offer. Register an easy-to-remember domain right now and point it to your real domain to make it easy for people to reach and remember you.

237. Organise the files on your computer and at the same time keep an eye out for strong or useful material that you had forgotten about. Maybe you have half-finished content for your site lying around, or some other part-complete project. You can now get back to work on this over the weekend, summer break or some other spare time you have on your hands.

238. Go to Google and search for your biggest competitor. Once you find out who links to your competitor's website, email those traffic forwarders and ask if they would also like to link to your site.

239. Gather all of your email contacts into a single folder so that you can send out a message with a really awesome offer to them tomorrow.

240. Do you have a customer that is difficult to get in touch with? Invite him/her to your next customer meeting or some other event. Let him/her present their company and increase your chances of getting closer to the customer.

241. It's time to do a SWOT-analysis. SWOT stands for Strengths, Weaknesses, Opportunities and Threats. Sit down with all the people in your company that have the information on how things are running and look at the finances, the daily work and the marketing. Are there any customers you are at risk of losing? What strengths can you build on? Can you trust that all your suppliers will indeed supply? Are there any openings anywhere that you haven't seen? This analysis may surprise you and could revitalise the entire company. At the same time it will show you how you can protect against your weaker areas.

242. Audit your customer register – you probably send out many letters and other things to the same lists you always use. A large part of your list – sometimes up to 50% of the names – will not be current anymore. Maybe they bought something only once and aren't really planning on buying anything else, or perhaps they've switched jobs and the letter no longer reaches them, or is thrown away.

Update your list using your order history. Who has bought something in the past year? Send your best material to them. Those who have bought something one or two years ago can get a cheaper version of your letters and brochures and see what results you get from that. Remove the rest of the names from your list.

243. Evaluate your memberships. Is everything you're a part of giving you something back? Do you get support, friends, education and customers? If the organisations you're a part of aren't helping you reach your goals then there's no sense in being a member – so take out the axe.

244. Make sure that you have an archive of your old newsletters on your website. It works as good content and also serves as a guarantee for new subscribers that there really is a letter and this isn't just a sneaky way to gather addresses.

245. Come up with an item that reminds customers to come back to your website and order more. It can be a mouse pad, a pen, a diary, or really anything, preferably with a customer number printed on it for future purchases.

I'm the perfect example of a customer that buys many things at different locations. Right now, for example, I'm studying to get a coast skipper's license for piloting ships and so I need a lot of maps. When I buy a map from a store I rarely remember what the web shop was called and so the next time I want to buy something, I have to start all over again. If the map shop had sent a pen with their name on it, they would have automatically received my next order because I would have had their website details there on the pen for reference.

246. Place this text snippet up in some appropriate places on your site:

> "It would be great to hear what you think about this. Send your comments straight to me at yourname@yourcompany.com"

This is good for so many reasons:

- You get feedback from your customers, helping you to change and improve things.

- You show everyone (not just those that write to you) that you have an active internet presence.

- You create a bond with all those who write to you, since you of course write back to them.

- You notice what captivates your website visitors and can do more of that.

There are probably a lot more reasons but these alone are enough for you to invest five minutes towards putting this text up wherever it may be appropriate.

247. Wherever you show a product have a button or some text that says "Order here" in close proximity to the product.

248. Ask your visitors what they would like you to write about on your site. Also, ask your customers what they would like you to write about.

249. Plan to make your website more automated. Why not add an offer request form that customers can fill out to get an instant quote? Why not start an automatic response service where customers can get your latest brochure sent by email?

250. Do a simple test with your pricing. Shamelessly double your hourly rates. Most people selling services underestimate their own worth, a symptom of the underdog perspective that many of them work with. I recommend that you double your hourly rates from whatever they are today. Think about it. Even if you lose half of your customers you will still earn the same money from the customers who stay. And the customers who stay are the ones that are really worth your time.

At Redaktionen we have done this on several occasions, most of all because we had too much to do, especially with holding courses, and needed to reduce our number of customers in order to have spare time for other things. We raised our daily prices on education from about $1300 to $3000 and, sure, a few customers disappeared, but new ones soon dropped in and eventually filled their spots. Higher prices also mean we can provide a higher quality of service.

251. If your business don't show up on Google, register your site again at:
www.google.co.uk/business/placesforbusiness

252. If your business'website is not ranked well by Google a quick trick is to add a few links on your site that contain your company's name. It often helps.

253. Bookmark your competitors' websites. Make a habit of reading these websites for about five minutes once a week.

254. Come up with five different places (other companies, other organisations, etc.) where your brochure should be available. Write down in your calendar a specific date when you will call them to suggest working together.

255. Analyse 50 of your customers and see what they have in common. New customers will most likely be very similar to your old customers. The more you know about the people you do business with now, the more you will know about the ones you'll do business with in the future.

256. Send an email to people that you would like to have as customers. It reminds them that you are accessible when they are ready to make a decision. A good way is to first publish information about something special on your website and then steer them there. And once they're there, give them a chance to contact you.

257. New habit – write in your calendar what time you will set aside to take care of administration work this week. Administration can be handled at times when customers are hard to reach. Why shuffle papers when there are customers you should meet?

258. Google yourself. If you're not already doing this every now and then you're crazy. This is about what other people see when they run a search on your name. Find out what customers, competitors and others say about your company. If you can, take part in the discussion to represent or defend your company. Every time a customer considers hiring you, you can bet they've run a Google search on you first.

259. Google other companies. Of course you can go to their websites, but it's more interesting and profitable to see what other people think about your competition and their partners. You can learn an incredible amount of things that you didn't already know about your potential new customers – and, of course, about your competitors as well.

260. Google your prospective clients. Imagine that you come across their values, ideologies and ways of thinking somewhere on the web. You can find their goals and dreams. This will give you an advantage when you eventually make contact with them. The prospects will get the feeling that you've really done your homework.

261. Decide to get a few new links every week. Set up a special time for it. For example, spend one hour every Thursday looking for new sites that would want to link to your site. There's no real end to this project and you will advance a bit every time you successfully add to it.

262. To market more expensive products, especially if they are new on the market, it is often more profitable for you if you split the price up into a "per-day price". Instead of telling the customers that something costs £5000, the price can now suddenly become a mere £13 per day (5000/365). A lot of new customers find this easier to digest and you will have an easier time selling it. Figure out your own per-day prices right now to put in your price lists and on your website.

263. Schedule a brainstorming meeting once a month in your calendar. Choose the day and time when you have the least things taking place and make it a finding-new-customers-only meeting.

264. Schedule a time when you will find new customers. Allocate two to ten hours a week to this and stick to it. Write this down for every week in your calendar right now.

265. Take some time to make a list of your top five dream customers and contact them. You might need more than five minutes for this, but get started on it now by making some initial notes for five minutes.

266. Send a test gift to your ten best customers along with an offer to buy something. Watch what happens. If it works on a small scale, try it on a bigger scale.

267. Think about flyers for a moment. If you were forced by law to pass out flyers for your company, what would it say on those flyers, where would you distribute them and to whom? When you know all this (it should take you less than five minutes to come up with) do it! Don't be a coward.

You could even stand in the parking lot outside of a big convention one day and personally pass out flyers to all the office supply managers, for example, and explain to them that your prices can't always compete with the giants but that you always do everything in your power for your customers.

268. Will it benefit your customers to frequently buy from you? No? In that case it's time to take five minutes to create a loyalty programme. It doesn't need to be complicated. You just have to decide what the regular customers should get from you for being loyal to your company. Then of course you also need to tell them about it.

It can be as simple as keeping track of the regular customers yourself and giving them discounts directly, or producing a customer card that entitles them to a discount (or more products for the same price). However you do it, do it now.

269. Make an advertising note in business card format with the top reasons why people should visit your website printed on both the front and the back. Then distribute this to people as if it was burning in your pocket.

270. Look over your important contact points for your customers. Do the people that visit you know you have a newsletter? Do the customers you talk with on the telephone know that you have a website where they can order whenever they want? Does it say in your information material that you will go through customers' needs on location for free? Simply put – where in your contact processes can you give the customers more information that brings them closer to you and your company? Take five minutes to answer this question and make a plan.

271. Create a document where you list all of your most obvious competitors in a single column and then start gathering information about each one of them – everything you can. Create a new email address that's not related to your company and subscribe to their newsletters. Ask them questions from your anonymous address. Be a sleuth and get all the information that you need. Order their brochures and all of their information material. Order their products if you can. Ask someone to call and complain to them. Do everything that a detective would.

272. Create "How to" articles. Learn from magazines and put together several of your own articles that give readers answers to how they could achieve something in ten steps.

273. Write down one small and one large reward that you will give yourself. The small reward you will get when you have reached a halfway point or interim goal and the big reward comes when you have accomplished a huge goal at the end of the next month, six months or year. Keep a note about these rewards somewhere where you will notice it often.

274. What newspapers do your customers read? Find out. Maybe it is fairly obvious which types of media they consume and in that case it's probably also true for potential future customers. Why not phone those places and arrange to place an ad that says something like:

"Wanted – finder's fee offered.

Five companies that match the following:

(Here you describe the profile of your ideal customer.)

If you fit this description – and are one of the first five who calls – then you get a free X and also a Y in our limited time offer. Call now! There are only five slots to fill."

---

275. Become a member at WebmasterWorld (webmasterworld.com) – it's a cool place for internet nerds and there's a tremendous amount of knowledge gathered there on everything to do with the internet.

If you need a new web designer – search there. If you need a new technician – anyone that knows a thing or two can be found there. It's free to join! When you've become a member, mark a day in your calendar when you will visit the site and learn things.

Translate your terms and conditions from legal babble into normal English

Find a brochure that you either created yourself or one that was sent to you. Take a look at the language in it. Does it feel like you, or whoever wrote the text, was writing to their best friend? Probably not. It's probably written in an impersonal way for an unidentified mass of people. To a certain extent, it's probably written to show how smart the writer is. This doesn't really appeal to the customer.

To me it feels impersonal, boring and is more of a testimony to a lack of self-confidence that the sender is trying to compensate for with big words and complicated explanations. Know-it-alls, my grandmother would have said.

You can see this kind of thing everywhere. Writing in this way you are creating a barrier in the hunt for new customers because the only people who fully understand this kind of lingo are you and your competitors, and other people who are in one way or another connected to your line of business.

This matter is extremely important for both your old and new customers because they want to feel that your company will be a resource for them. What if a new customer's very first encounter with your company results in them suddenly understanding what your complex world is all about, simply because you explained it in a way they could understand? It is especially worth you doing this if you sell something that normally seems a bit complicated.

The best part is that you will probably be quite alone in it too. When your competitors see your simplified material they will think you phrased things too simplistically and unprofessionally.

Customers don't care about how smart you think you are. They only care about what you or what your product/service can do for them.

Make your text:

- Memorable
- Easy to understand
- Easy to explain to others.

Does that sound hard? It's really not. The only thing you need to do is pretend that a customer is sitting in front of you, saying: "Tell me in a simple way what you can do for me."

Try this out immediately! There is no time to lose in making your business concept easier for the world to understand. Phrase your entire business idea in a single sentence so that anyone can understand why your company exists and what you can help your customers with.

Part 6

100 Effective Ways To Sell More From Your Site

276. Visit your main competitor's website and pay attention to whatever causes that stabbing feeling in your stomach (there's always something). This feeling is called jealousy and it's a good indication of what these people seem so good at that you need to do more of yourself.

277. Visit your website and pretend to be a stressed out customer that wants to buy three different things. How easy docs it feel to order? Now imagine the customer gets grumpy and wants to ask a question about the product. Is it easy? If it's hard, what can you do now to make it easier for the customer to buy/contact you?

278. Visit your webpage as an uncertain customer that just discovered your company. He has never ordered anything online before but is curious. Are you making him feel more secure by telling him more about your company somewhere (he wants to order but is unsure of who you are)?

279. If you have good information on your business, do you also provide good information on how much products cost, how you ship them and how long the customer can expect to wait for their delivery?

280. Go to your website as a first-time customer. She likes your site and probably wants to order something eventually but not right now. Are you catching this opportunity by letting her subscribe to a newsletter that will inform her of when you have a sale?

281. Do you ask for more information than you need when people are using your site? If someone is subscribing to your newsletter, it's quite enough to get their email address. If someone wants to buy something from you then it's enough to only ask for whatever you need to know to get the products to the customer and an email address for a receipt and confirmation to be sent to.

282. Put text your website that says "Ask about this product" followed by an email address. That way you can catch customers who feel unsure.

283. What do the product pictures on your website look like? Do you have good-quality pictures that show your products/services in use? Do you have photos of your manufacturing process? Could you give a virtual tour of your office or factory and show an exciting work environment? Turn this into a competition to make it more interesting, with questions about what was seen in the tour.

If you can do this quickly and easily then get your camera and do it. It adds an extra feature to your website that visitors will like. If you need a professional to help then contact a photographer right away.

284. Research affiliate programmes and see if this could be something that would work for you. An affiliate programme is really a kind of reselling program where other sites get paid for sending traffic to you through showing what you sell on your site. If that leads to a final sale, the referrer will receive a percentage of the profits on the order.

To find a technical platform that works for you search for affiliate programmes on Google. You will find separate solutions and also companies that specialise in affiliate programmes where you don't even have to move a muscle yourself.

285. Create or find an appropriate list of common terms or jargon within your area of expertise and put it on your website as a glossary. Then tell the sector magazines that those who are interested in knowing what certain words mean can visit your site. You are turning yourself into an expert.

Lists of words and expressions are also great because you can include important keywords within them. On one of my own sites, **www.starta-eget.se**, you can see how I've added a word list that's all about business management. A lot of the words in my list rank as number one on many search engines.

286. Plan to make a hook page, or a series of these pages. Hook pages provide tips on how to use your products and related content. The benefit here is that you show you are so committed to what you do that you add new dimensions to it.

Think of an example of a retailer of camping accessories. They might create a hook page showing amazing camping locations. It's not only easy to make visitors like that list; it's also easy to write a press release about it in connection with the release of your latest tent. You can allow newspapers or journals to publish the entire list, as long as they include a reference to where it comes from.

287. Add a question page. If you want to increase customer confidence and create interaction with readers you can have a page with questions about your area of expertise and encourage visitors to your site to ask questions for you to answer. If no questions are submitted, think about what your most commonly asked questions are and answer these on the page.

288. Call someone you know who's looking for a little extra work. Ask them to visit your site and to do the things that you would like your visitors to do. For example, the person could pretend to be a first-time visitor looking for more information on the things you sell and how to best obtain them. Analyse the results.

289. Have coupons that people can print out and use in your physical shop. Create an email list that visitors join to find out when new coupons will be made available on the website. Since you'll now have their email addresses, this also makes it very simple to create a customer club to which special offers and discounts are sent out at regular intervals.

290. Entice customers who have already put one item in their shopping cart with a bonus if they order one more product (or two more, or five more). Think about which products you can add little extras to if the customer buys them. If you can do this for all of your products – awesome! It works! Your bonus products should of course be desirable, of high quality and have a high perceived value for the customer.

291. Tell customers what others have bought. One technique that you have surely seen before is to show what other customers have purchased in addition to the item you are about to buy. It works well if the suggestion feels closely related to the purchase. I think it often feels like the products that "others have bought" are just randomly picked and/or made up, so ensure any suggestions you make are realistic if you use this technique on your website.

292. You can offer customers a better price if they buy two instead of just one. Remind the customer that the item just placed in the shopping cart will be cheaper if a larger quantity is purchased in the same order.

293. Encourage impulse shopping. You have surely impulsively shopped yourself when you've been close to the checkouts in stores. A pair of socks, filters for your coffee maker, or just a chocolate bar.

Does the same concept apply to an internet shop? Absolutely. And it's actually much easier. A person has to take far more steps to the checkout in a physical store than they do on the internet. The only thing you need to do on a website is place an enticing product on the ordering page and a box customers can tick if they want to, for example, "try this new cleaning spray for only £9.50". In the store, people need to reach out and grab different products, but on the internet impulse buying can happen with just a single click.

294. Offer the possibility for customers to ask questions. Your customer has bought something and was considering maybe buying something else too but they weren't entirely sure it was the right choice. Make it easy for them to ask questions during this process.

295. When you send an order confirmation letter or email to your customers make sure to include a recommendation link. If a customer was impressed by their experience with you there is a high possibility they will want to recommend you to their friends. Make sure this is easy for them to do. The point when a customer has just bought something is the time when they are most likely to want to tell others about it.

296. Special offers sell. Make sure to have a special offer on your website and tell all employees to have the address for the page showing the offer in their email signatures.

297. Increase trust quickly by placing customer reviews and notices about warranties next to your products. Many companies guarantee things but fail to show this as clearly as they ought too. Undecided customers like to see guarantees from the manufacturer or retailer, and feedback from previous customers. It's easier for you to sell to those who have never heard of your company if potential customers can easily see the positive views of others who have bought from you.

Customer reviews – where to place them

- Underneath your product pictures.
- Next to your promises to customers.
- In the margins of your pages.
- In appropriate areas during the checkout process.
- As links in the product descriptions.

298. You should definitely place your special offers on your homepage, but remember to also place them on your other most-visited pages.

299. When you optimise your website and add keywords to it don't just rely on the most popular phrases used by competitors whose websites all have the same goal as yours. Try as well to find some less frequently used search phrases and pull in a few visitors with these.

300. Do you have any good stories about your company and how you helped someone that you can mention on your website? Visitors will like to read things like this and what is liked by website visitors is of course also appreciated by search engines. If you do have stories like this take time to put them on your website and in your printed brochures.

301. Autoresponders are a fantastic feature that allows you to offer a service to your customers around the clock. It works like this: when someone sends an email to an address with an autoresponse activated, it automatically sends a reply with a pre-written message. You probably knew this already. And if you knew about it, you have probably already used it as well. But how have you used it?

Autoresponses are often used by people who want to explain that they've gone away on vacation, that they're sick, or on a business trip. I have rarely seen anyone use autoresponders in a truly clever way. Vacations, illness, business trips – what a waste of a great marketing tool.

With the help of autoresponse you can make special information about your company, products, services and marketing material completely accessible around the clock for everybody. But you can do that anyway right? That's true, but with autoresponse you'll also get the email address of the person who requested the information and benefit even more by sending them a follow-up letter to them later on. You can create some particularly attractive material that people can only get access to through autoresponse.

The cool thing about this is that you can offer services around the clock, so when your office is closed customers will still get a response from you. The customers also get exactly what they want; it's a win-win situation. It's also easy to set up and easy to change.

You can start a ten-week class that runs completely automatically. You can provide in-depth information down to the smallest molecule about your products. Can you see the potential in this?

302. Offer your customers a free e-class on something and see how many take the bite. If enough people show an interest you can then create the material for this class. One thing that makes the internet so great is that it's so easy and low-risk to try things out.

303. If people tend to misspell key phrases in your line of business then register a domain name with the wrong spelling and point that to your main site. A certain amount of people still search for things online by typing addresses in their web browser instead of using a search engine.

304. If you have text on your site that says things like this: "Read more about our services, click here" then get your calendar out right away and schedule some time to change it to more specific links where you'll write something more exciting instead. For example "Read more about how you can motivate yourself and others" (this example might lead to details about a class on motivational techniques).

305. Take a look at one of your website's sub-pages. Is the language very formal or technical? If that's the case, is it appropriate in relation to who your clients are, or is the language too difficult for them? If you can, simplify it. Schedule time to take care of this.

306. Explain to the visitors on your site why they should do whatever it is that you want them to do. If your site is full of passive suggestions, fix it. People – you and I included – respond to calls to action and often do what we are enticed to do as long as we have a good reason to do it.

307. Look for proof that what you sell is really as good as you say it is. You may be selling financial services and a well-respected magazine writes that companies who hire accounting firms are required to pay less in back taxes. Tell visitors to your own site, subscribers to your newsletters or your followers on Twitter what the magazine wrote – this promotes your service.

308. Look at your offers and ask yourself how you can make them easier to understand. Visitors to your site must be given the chance to weigh up what you are selling. Otherwise they will be too scared to buy. Don't complicate things.

309. Check the text on your website – are you sticking to the rule of making a single point in each paragraph?

Good. If you're not, then this needs to be changed so that you don't make it hard for visitors to read your content. Your site already has a tough job keeping your visitors interested. Never make things harder than they need to be.

310. Do an experiment with the text on your site. Play around with metaphors and analogies. Try it out on a single page today and see what happens. It will usually make the text feel more alive while at the same time making it easier for your visitors to understand what you're selling.

I love to see examples that make complicated things easier to understand. For example, the word "wattage" doesn't really mean a lot to me and I don't have any particular desire to learn about it either, but if someone is trying to sell me a gadget with twice the wattage and states "It's like trading in your old Fiat for a new Ferrari" then I'll understand why it's better (and will have an easier time selling the idea to my wife).

311. Cut down on the babble. Can you say the same thing with half the text? Try it out on one of your product pages. Your customers are in a hurry!

312. Make a plan for how you are going to keep your website updated regularly with new content. It makes both customers and search engines happy. Why not take out your calendar and devote some of those slow summer days at work to writing content for the fall season. Do the same thing for Christmas. The best sites plan their content weeks and months ahead.

313. Do you cheat to get traffic to your website? It may work at the moment but make plans to remove all the cheats from your pages. The search engines are always on the hunt for abusers and you can't win like this in the long run.

314. Do you have too many choices on one page? Steer visitors where you want them to go, don't try to tell them about everything on the same page.

315. Do you have contact information on every page? Make sure you put this in place if you haven't already.

316. Lose the contact forms. If someone wants more information about something that Wayne at your company knows, why not put up contact information (email address, phone number, etc.) straight to Wayne instead? Or at least give the visitor the chance to contact Wayne without using a generic form.

317. Add a News page to your website. If your company regularly has new news to share, then you can date the posts. If you only come up with something new every six months you shouldn't date the entries because it will make it seem like you stopped updating your page. Smart companies don't miss the chance to market new products in this way.

318. What kind of pictures do you use on your site? Is it stock images with smiling businessmen and women in different situations? Well, it's better than nothing. If the pictures are stolen from other sites then remove them immediately. They can create big problems when you least expect it. Why not take your own pictures instead? Let your staff be part of it.

319. Back up your entire site at least once a month. Schedule it into your calendar for the whole year and in the last entry you'll write "pass this on to next year". I was lazy with this and lost a lot of material, wasting time and energy, during the dark month of March 2009. I don't want to say any more about it because I feel like an idiot. Don't make the same mistake I did.

320. Try changing the sales links on your site to a bold style or a bigger format for a week to see if more people click on them.

321. Is there a reason for your visitors to take action on every page of your website? If not, give them a reason to do so in at least two places on every page. Tell them to buy something, subscribe to your free newsletter, call you or visit you, read a related article – anything that brings them closer to you.

322. Send an offer for a new purchase with order confirmation emails – surprise customers by making it a really great offer. It could be for a complementary product to fit with their existing purchase. If they act quickly it can be sent along with their main purchase. The only thing customers will need to do to take you up on the offer is click on a link. Make the offer so awesome that the customer simply can't refuse to snatch it up.

323. Check the statistics on what visitors most often search for that take them to your website (it may surprise you which words come up) and strengthen these areas of your website so that you can sell more. You can do this through linking these keywords with more of your content or with direct links from these pages to products or services that you would like customers to look at more closely.

324. Put text on your website that encourages visitors to give feedback. It's so easy to become blinded by your own perspective and if you can get your visitors' opinions for free then make sure you welcome these views.

325. Check your opening sentences on every sub-page where you sell things. Does the text engage and pull the reader in? If not then change it, or make plans to change it when you have more time.

326. Visit Google and search for the phrases that you believe your customers would use in order to find what you offer. Look at the first five results because that's where you want to be found. Are you there?

It's great if you're already there, but if not you can quickly visit the other sites that are and see what they do in order to be so high up on the list. If they aren't in direct competition with you, but rather complement your products, you can send an email to the most appropriate person at each company saying something like this:

"Hello Lisa,

"I visited your site today and was really impressed. I work with X and thought maybe we could work together in some way. You are welcome to look around on my site and if interested I hope you'll get back to me.**"**

327. Write something positive about a company that you like (and want to work with) on your website. Tell them what you have done and ask them if they would perhaps like to work with you (or even just return the favour and write about you on their site).

328. Put up a notice on your site to say that those who link to your website will take part in a lottery for a prize of one of your finest products or a lottery scratch card. You could even place an advert for this in a relevant publication or on another relevant website. This is how it's done:

> **"**Add a link to our website on your own site and write to linkcontest@yourcompany.com to tell us where your link is – you will be entered into a prize draw. The winner is drawn at the end of every month and will be presented on this page. Good luck!**"**

Don't fuss about links not being good enough just because they're from a site you perceive to be minor. Treat all links equally.

329. Time how long it takes to read the most important page on your website. Check your statistics and see how long your customers stay on that particular page. If they leave right away, or in much less time than it takes to read the page, it could be because the page is overly rambling or boring. Change it.

330. Have you described your guarantees on your website? How do you do it – with long incoherent babble, or with a few simple points that show you are on the customer's side? Simplify your complicated guarantees – if for no other reason than to just see if it results in a sales increase.

331. Do you have a short "About this company" page? If not, you need to make one and put up a photo of yourself and other staff right away. That's the first step. When you have more time on your hands, you can put a picture of all of your employees with their respective responsibilities and maybe a few personal facts under the pictures. Many people (I'm one of them) like to see that there are real people behind the web addresses before they get right down to it and buy, contact, subscribe, or whatever else you want visitors to your website to do.

332. Have you described your website's internal links clearly? If not, do it so that the visitors know exactly where they are heading and get what they expected when they clicked the link. Otherwise you face the risk of them getting irritated and just leaving your website.

333. Check your statistics and see which page your visitors mostly leave your website from. What is it with that page? Maybe it is the most logical place to leave the site from, which is fine. But if not then you just got valuable information on a possible weak link on your site. Make adjustments to the page if these are needed.

334. Check up on whether your web host is really doing their job. I think that web hosts are generally bad at notifying you when your site is down, which happens sometimes. For me there have been several nightmarish days when several sites were down and the web host didn't bother to explain what was happening. Keep a check on your websites yourself.

If you create an account with a service such as SiteUptime (**siteuptime.com**), Service Uptime (**serviceuptime.com**), Netcraft (**uptime.netcraft.com**) or **host-tracker.com** will you get continuous information about how often your sites can't be seen by visitors. The starting packages are free and you will receive reports automatically, so you won't have to bother with manual checking.

335. If you have good content, put a short note under every article on your website to say that other sites can publish the same information if they link back to you. This is an easy way to get links from other sites.

336. Make a favicon. This is the symbol that is shown next to your website's name or address in web browsers and bookmark lists. If you rely on the default symbols you will easily disappear among those that have many different sites bookmarked. Your web designer can help you create a favicon or there are many free services online that can help.

337. If you sell things online, throw in a brochure with a special offer that is easy to take advantage of with every single order that goes out to customers.

338. Do you know someone who is really good at spelling and grammar? Ask that person to look over your website and identify any mistakes.

339. Rewrite the text on your website. Sadly we often tend to trust our suppliers' own texts and copy them straight from their material because we might be a little lazy or because we believe they actually put some intelligent thought into it. Don't take that for granted. Pretend that it is your best friend who's going to read your website. Once this is done customers who visit your site will instinctively feel that your company is approachable and relatable.

340. Write all the title tags on the most important pages of your website in caps. That will make your site stick out more in the search results. A title tag is what tells search engines and internet users what your website is about – they help people decide whether to visit your site.

341. You might consider writing the title tags for your website with a blank space between each letter. It's unconventional, maybe, but it will make them stand out in search results.

342. Change the description tags on your best pages to something more interesting. The description tag is where you tell people what the page is about. It's often the reason people click on the page so make it striking and informative.

343. Add some new keywords to the title tags of the pages on your site that don't draw enough traffic. Make sure the words are also used on the page itself. Google doesn't like pages that try to draw traffic using keywords that don't have any relevance to the page itself.

344. If your company primarily works in the local market, make sure that the name of the town where you are located is on your website and in your title tags.

345. Go to your website and compare your best-selling product with whatever sells the least. Is there something to learn about the page introducing your best-selling product that you can try on your least sold product? I'm thinking about presentation, enthusiasm in the text, the price and how it makes you feel inside when you read about the product.

We often focus even more attention on the products we sell the most of and that's good, but at the same time we tend to sometimes treat those products that aren't working so well rather coldly.

346. What do you help people with? Make sure that it's written clearly in the first paragraph (not the third or fourth) on your website as well as all printed material.

347. Give away something for free on your site that could be received by email. It can be informative material or something fun that's related to your area of expertise.

348. If you don't have a newsletter because you're not convinced that it will give you something back, try putting a note on the home page of your website saying "subscribe to our newsletter to find out about our latest sales and offers" (or whatever you believe your visitors will be attracted too). This way you'll find out if anyone bites. If enough people do, then the argument is won – you must start a newsletter.

349. If you have a sub-page that doesn't draw a lot of people to it despite doing everything else right, it can be a good idea to change the word order in the title. If you have the title "Plumber in Seattle" you can try "Seattle – plumber" instead. I have done this with several of my pages with very good results.

350. Set up a watch service on your competitors using Google Alerts (**www.google.com/alerts**). If any news pops up about them you'll get an email about it.

351. If you have an info-address (e.g., info@your-company.com) on your site instead of a person's name, change it right now and more people will be inclined to get in touch.

352. Ask for content from your visitors. Ask people to write in and tell you about the best time they've had with your product. Hand out a prize. This can become an interesting little collection that will inspire new customers and let them know what your products are good for.

353. Run a search on Google for keywords relating to your products and services. Click on the paid advertisements and contact those who advertise there. Write a letter to them about a link exchange. The companies that advertise with Google are hungry for exposure and they may very well be interested in getting more marketing for free with your help. Instead of emailing to let them know you want to exchange links, you can contact them by telephone. This works wonders, believe me.

354. Sometimes when you ask people to do things they will be pleased to do so and all it costs you is asking the question. If you asked me to bookmark your web shop in my favourites then there is a very good chance that I would do so, if I could have a use for your products or services in the future. Encourage your visitors to put your web shop in their favourites so that they can easily come back to it. Also instruct them on how to do this if they aren't very internet savvy.

355. Try giving out lottery tickets to websites that link to you – and especially the sites that are relevant to your business. Add this text to your site:

> "Everyone who links to us and has a site within or somehow related to our area of business will receive lottery tickets. Please feel free to ask us how many lottery tickets a link from you is worth to us. Write to linkexchange@yourcompany.com."

356. Test one page of your website per day until you have checked them all, then start again. The model that works best is really very simple:

- Pose a problem to the visitors.

- Explain why this is a problem for the visitor.

- Show in an elegant way how your product takes care of this problem – make sure that the customer wants more of whatever you offer.

- Show the reader how to take the next simple step in getting it.

Do all of your pages look like this?

357. Put several links to other important sites on your own website before you ask those sites if they would like to link back to you. Consider writing a short positive sentence about that company under the link and show this to the owner of the site you're linking to. They should be flattered by the compliment and they will hopefully want to link back to you.

Create a web policy in five minutes

There's something about websites that gives them a tendency to end up sliding towards the bottom of the priority list, if not last on the list. The real world is always poking you for your attention while websites generally remain fairly silent. After all, your site isn't a live salesperson that tells you that the brochures need to be updated because they are obsolete. This syndrome must be met head-on by having a clear policy for your web presence.

Start with formulating the purpose for the website clearly and then stick to it. This is how your ten commandments should look:

1. The website's first and foremost job is to generate more sales.

2. We shall be personal but not private.

3. All our new material should first strengthen the will of the visitor to buy and secondly make them want to subscribe to our newsletter.

4. Every page should support one of our product groups – the one which sells best.

5. All of our pages should invite the visitor to contact us.

6. Our web shop is never finished. There are always new things to do that can encourage customers to decide to buy something.

7. The web shop will be updated once a week/month.

8. Content and development should be discussed at a meeting every [set a particular day and time for this].

9. All great ideas that help strengthen the web shop should be rewarded with X.

10. Employee NN is responsible for the web shop.

Set up this list as a document or email and be sure to distribute it to all concerned parties.

Test your MWR (Most Wanted Response) in five minutes

You want your customers to do something specific when they visit your site, right? You want them to buy, order a brochure, find out where the nearest dealer is, or simply contact you.

If you build your entire site around the goal of what you want the customer to do, he/she will end up doing it a lot more often. It sounds quite obvious, but if you look at your own site can you honestly say it's built around one super clear aim? Not many can say that.

The idea behind MWR is to answer the customer's question "What can you do for me?" at the same time as propelling the customer on towards whatever you want him/her to do for you. This is good for both parties.

The really successful websites have a sequence of perhaps two, or in some cases three, MWRs, depending on priority.

For example:

- MWR 1 – They want you to buy something or to fill out a form so that they can contact you.

... but if you don't want to do that then

- MWR 2 – They want you to subscribe to their newsletter.

...and if you don't want to do that then

- MWR 3 – They want you to add their site to your favourites.

Now it's your turn.

These questions are designed to help you figure out which MWR is right for your site:

- What do I want to remind my customers to do on my site – what's the goal?
- How can my MWR help my visitors reach their goals?
- How can I measure how effective my MWR is?
- How can I improve my MWR for better results?

When you have answered all of these questions it's probably time for you write something new, rewrite something old, expand your content or rebuild something on your site so that all of your content supports your MWR.

Perhaps you need to place a contact link on every page or make links to your newsletter more visible throughout the whole site – everything depends on your own reasons for running your website. And all this is of course not about tricking your customers into doing things, but about helping them reach their goals, whilst at the same time reaching your own.

Part 7

Improving Your Website

358. Immediately add a discount system to your website if you have not already done this.

You can, for example, do what we do at Redaktionen – we reward customers that buy a number of items with a discount. Those who buy at least two books get a discount. Check out **www.redaktionen.se** to see how it works.

359. Make your websites printable if you know your customers are likely to want to print out the information they find there. Make sure that it's also easy to see on the paper where the information came from so that the customer does not forget your website.

360. Make sure that your logo links back to the welcome page if someone clicks on it. This makes it easy for customers to get back to your homepage again.

361. If you have a search function for your site implement some form of statistics feature so that you can see what people are searching for. If a term that is searched for a lot does not yield any results, see to it that the word they are searching for does return something.

I have made the mistake myself of not understanding this. On my website, **www.starta-eget.se**, there were many people who searched for "the financial report method". Before I understood this, they were always getting "Your search for this word returned no results" as the answer to their search, which is not conducive to getting sales from these customers.

If you don't have a search function on your site then have one included right away. It doesn't matter if your site is a mere three pages of content – you will still get useful information on what visitors are looking for and you can develop the site further according to what they want.

362. Do you have a site map to make it easier for visitors to navigate your site and also for search engines to see and follow all links? That will make it easier for Google and other search engines and will ensure your pages have the best chance of being indexed by search engines (which means the search engines have registered your site and collected and stored data ready for people to search for it).

Your sitemap should be text-based so that users can find their way back if they somehow get lost. And make sure that the sitemap can be reached from all pages.

363. Make your 404 page useful. A 404 page is an HTTP standard response code indicating that a page wasn't found on your site – make sure that your 404 page links to your homepage or your sitemap.

364. Make sure your order forms store information and pass this back to you even if someone hasn't filled them in fully or correctly. The most important thing is for you to receive a correct email address. If any of the other details are missing or wrong then at least you can get in touch with the person to collect the rest of their details.

Why do this? Quite simply because you still want to take orders even from people who may not want to bother with filling out your form according to strict criteria. If there are too many "required fields" then customers may lose interest. Don't stop customers from giving you their money because of this.

365. Make sure you always have text links. You may think it's cooler to use image links but then you've successfully blocked customers that have turned that function off in their browsers.

366. Put more internal links on the different pages of your site. It helps visitors to get to your most important pages.

367. Give your sub-pages real names. If for example your site is about cakes you should have the word "cakes" in the title of the page and not www.yourdomain.com/dssfdf3article.htm. Search engines like pages that are named after their content.

368. Go to Google and enter the following in the search bar: "link:www.yourownsitesname.com". You will get a number of hits that tell you how many people link to your website. Write "Number of links – X" in your calendar for today, then skip two months ahead and write: "Run a link check – look two months back". What you will find out this way is whether all of your hard work with your website is actually paying off over time. What you want is of course for the number of links to be increasing with time.

369. Show your products on the welcome page of your site. Many companies make the mistake of not doing this and instead use their start page as some sort of presentation.

370. Do you have manuals for your products? Put them on your website.

371. Catch the names of those who are about to leave your site by use of an exit page. Here it is very important to come up with a super duper important reason to register. They were on their way out and here you come and bother them – you have to make it worth the customer's time to want to stay and give you their email address.

372. Connect your site to Facebook so that people can 'Like' it (**www.facebook.com/insights**).

373. Exchange subscription boxes with complementary sites. Their customers can subscribe to your newsletter and your customers to theirs.

374. Start a survey on your site. For instance, if you sell health products you can ask the question: Do you trust the advice of doctors in the newspapers? If you run a store selling CDs and books, why not ask visitors what they have enjoyed recently, or if they agree with the critics' views on a particular release? You are involving people in your website and learning about your customers.

375. Put your most important information so that it's always visible on your site without needing to scroll up, down or sideways. Imagine your visitors having very short attention spans and show them what they are looking for straightaway.

376. Make your welcome page small – preferably 50 KB or less. That way it will load quickly. If you don't know how big a page on your site is simply go to it and right click it. If you're using, for example, Firefox you click 'Show Site Info'. If you use Internet Explorer you would click on Properties. Other browsers will have this capability too.

377. Copy this text and edit it so that it fits your service and put it on your website:

■ What happens when you order?
"When you place an order from this site, it goes straight to [staff name], who packs it. We try to ship all orders on the day we get them and we use priority mail so that you get your orders quickly."

■ What happens if you are not satisfied?

"We want satisfied customers who will come back and visit us again, so we won't be fussy if you aren't satisfied with something you've ordered from us. You always have X days to return our products and that means you can send back anything you don't want. The only thing you would pay for is the return shipping."

(I want to show you what your customers are worried about and how you can address those concerns in a more personal way. Many companies are armed to the teeth with many bullet points to protect themselves, which gives customers the feeling they're an enemy that the company needs to be on guard against. Don't do that. Show customers that you're kind.)

378. Show your visitors how many products are left. There is no better way to get your visitors to act quickly. If you can't connect your site to your stock database, it's still a good idea to warn customers when the product is close to being sold out.

379. Put your telephone number on all the pages throughout the ordering process. If a customer gets stuck they can phone you with their order instead.

380. Put a bestsellers list that shows your top selling products/services on your site. Link directly to your products/services. Your visitors are automatically drawn to things that others have bought.

381. Look at your start page. Does it show clearly that people can buy from your website? If it doesn't, make sure you show the visitors that they can shop online. Some visitors don't know or don't consider the fact they might be able to buy from you directly. If you have dealers and want to avoid competing with them then make sure that you have direct links to their order pages.

382. Is it possible to view bigger pictures of the products on your site? If not, make sure that your web designer sees to it. The visitors want to get as close to the product as possible to feel comfortable about making the purchase.

383. Do your subscription boxes contain positive words? You can for example write:

> **"**Subscribe to our free/great/essential/useful/vital/interesting newsletter on [subject of your business].**"**

384. Visit your website and see if it's possible to reach anything at all on the site in three clicks or less. If not, find a solution.

385. Install Google analytics (**www.google.com/analytics**) on your site. It takes five minutes. Then take some time to see what kinds of information you can get from this service. There is a guide to using Google Analytics on the website.

386. Learn to write great titles for pages on your site, email newsletter and brochure. The job of the title is to make the reader curious about reading more. A good title draws the readers in and sells the rest of the text. It's extremely important if you want your customers to be interested in what you have to say. Tips on how to write good titles are:

- Give the reader a promise – "How to write a good title."

- Make a claim – "This is why titles are so important."
- Question something – "Do your titles really work?"
- Stand out – "How to write badass titles."

387. Your visitors do not all use the same web browser. More and more people are leaving Internet Explorer behind and moving to, for example, Firefox, Opera, Chrome and many others. This is why it's a good idea to find out what your site looks like when viewed through all of the different web browsers that exist.

You can check this very easily at Browser Shots (**browsershots.org**) by typing your web address in the search box at the beginning of the site, choosing which web browsers you want to view the site in (the most common ones are already checked) and then click "submit". Then you just wait a moment for the results. To help you choose which web browsers to view your site in, look through your statistics and find out which web browsers are most commonly used by your visitors.

388. Take your top three best-selling products/services and spend five minutes criticising them. Be an angry customer who has objections to buying from you and figure out the best possible answers to this visitor's questions. Make notes on how you would counter these objections.

Once you've done this, you will have a rough draft for text to write and put next to the products/services on your site. You can put a link next to the product/service that says:

This way you will give your potential customers an answer to their objections as they are buying.

389. Look for dead links on your site for free with **validator.w3.org/checklink**. Then ask your web developer to correct any problems.

390. Customers want your web pages to load quickly. Find out how fast they load using Pingdom (**tools.pingdom.com**). Again, ask your web developer to improve anything that is not satisfactory.

391. Add this line to the order form on your website: "How did you hear about us?"

392. Is there a sector registry for the line of business you are in? Is there a link to your website there? Do your country's business information pages have a link to your company?

393. Register as a user of Google's Webmaster Tools to get several great new tools and analyses of how Google views your site with direct suggestions for changes and improvements. **www.google.com/webmasters**

394. Go synonym hunting. Take a few minutes to write down as many synonyms for what you're selling as you can and give these to your webmaster (if you don't have a webmaster you keep the note yourself) and tell him/her that you want these words and concepts displayed on your site. If you need inspiration go to your competitors' sites and see how they describe what they do.

395. And lastly – visit your website "for the first time." View it as a brand new visitor would. How does it look? What do you need to do to improve it?

An Experiment

Do an exciting experiment right now. Before you begin, I need to say DON'T read the list of bullet points that follow on below. This is part of the experiment. Instead just go straight to your website right now and stay on its first welcome page for ten seconds.

When you have done this, read the following:

- What did you see first?
- Could you understand what the site was about without scrolling down the page or clicking on anything?
- Have you seen similar pages before elsewhere?
- If you were forced to come up with something that was missing, what would it be?

By answering these questions quickly and spontaneously you can see what needs to happen on your site to make it better. It may be enough to just make a few items bigger or change some pictures around. Or maybe be more direct in how you address visitors so that they know they've come to the right place.

If any of the necessary changes will take less than five minutes then do it right now. Otherwise add them to your "to do" list.

Finally, A Revelation

Most of the points in this book can be put into action in five minutes, but I hope that you will see their potential enough to want to put even more time into them.

Telling myself that tasks only take *five minutes* is a trick that I use every day to get myself started. If something feels a bit boring (for example, proofreading a website) I tell myself that all I have to do today is spend five minutes on it. And then I do exactly that. Before long my opposition to working is gone and suddenly, before I know it, I've finished the whole task. When I look down at my watch, the five minutes I set out to invest have usually turned into well over an hour.

Here's a final suggestion:

Choose ten things from this book and get started on them right now. You have five minutes to make the selection...

Bonus Articles

At the website **www.the5minutemarketer.com** you can read five-minute articles on all of these topics:

- 10 things that your customers are worried about
- 10 tips on how to give your customers an offer they can't refuse
- 10 tips on how to market successfully
- 17 things you should think about before you write to your customer
- 6 simple things that help you find new customers
- 7 things that help you help customers choose your company
- 8 reasons why so many fail with advertisement
- 8 important questions that help you with marketing
- 9 reasons why you and I and everyone else buys stuff
- Addressed direct advertisement – how to succeed with it
- Everyone who hates standing in line, raise their hand!
- Everyone is selling – you too
- Everything starts outside the store – how to get your customers inside
- To meet objections in the right way and thus sell more
- To succeed with sales demands that you stop making excuses
- Keeping your customers – how you do it
- Be more effective at conventions
- Selling in your store – how to sell more next month
- Selling in your store – how you charge for service

- Selling in your store – get rid of the signs
- Selling in your store for real professionals
- Selling in your store means to go with the flow
- The two most important ingredients for how to bake a good salesperson
- Get higher levels of self-confidence in being a salesperson
- Get customers to like you – to sell services
- Cutting the grass = marketing
- Make your customers into co-conspirators
- How you get your customers in the boat with you
- How you get customers to stop "thinking about it"
- How you get customers to not have time to consider your competition
- How to get newspapers to write about you
- How you make customers dependent on you
- How you make selling announcements
- How to kick the competition's butt
- How you show the customers that you care
- How you get publicity – media's own point of view
- How someone gets closer to journalists in the wrong way
- How the media defines a newspiece
- Cold calling – this is how you do it
- Competition analysis – how you do it simply
- Customer feedback in marketing – the road to the real money
- The solution to the puzzle of marketing is revealed!
- Marketing through social media
- Porter's five powers model

- Positioning – an expression that it pays to know about
- PR = have opinions, stand for something
- PR school for the insane
- Reference deals – how to create them
- Things you will not do while you are selling on the phone
- Write a sales letter – this is how you do it
- Stop selling – start helping
- Are you wasting your time on the wrong customer?
- Smart tips for how you lift yourself up as a salesperson when times are bad
- Butter the customers – or?
- A star salesperson – and how to create one
- How you advertise for your shop
- How to get free advertising
- How to get the customer over the threshold of doubt into buying
- How to get the customer to stay
- How to give your publicity a longer shelf life
- How to handle super annoying, even completely hopeless customers
- How to close more deals as a salesperson
- How to stop doing things for free
- Sow now and reap later
- This is how things would look if you took care of your business like a politician
- This is how you sell more to the customers in your shop
- Sell the right way
- Selling in a bad economy – tips and advice

- Selling more over the phone
- Salespeople – why don't you ever celebrate?
- Search engine optimising tips
- Tips for those who want to open up a shop
- Tips for those who want to sell more leading up to Christmas
- What are core values? Here's the answer
- Normal sales mistakes – do you do this?
- Show the customers right away who your products are meant for
- The world's easiest way to earn more money
- Are you like a £10 chocolate bar?
- Increase your sales by 42.5% in one year with our amazing product – just BS?
- Increase turnover in the shop by 50% next week
- Recession survival tips
- 10 reasons for why you should find other people to work with
- To think about this particular year
- A magic pill that lifts your company up immediately
- How you keep your focus on what you should be doing
- How you get everyone to like you
- How you get customers to recommend you to their friends
- How you get boring things done
- How you get everything you want done – without problems
- What you should do when you get angry at a customer
- How you stop putting things off

- How you take care of yourself when sales stop

- How you win everything with just a note in your pocket

- How you make a professional impression

- How you work with better focus and have more time left over

- How salespeople trick themselves

- How do you know your marketing is working as you want it to?

- Work smarter after vacations

- Can you set boundaries? If not, we will show you how

- Let technology work for your company

- Motivate yourself

- Personal efficiency 2.0

- Get better control over marketing

- Are you throwing away your time on the wrong customer?

- Smart things to do during downtimes

- Sleep better for good health

- Don't worry about your "to do" list – make a "do not do" list instead

- This is how you make a good impression on your first customer meeting

- This is how you find new customers

- This is how you stay on top as a company owner every day

- This is how you tell bad news in a good way

- This is how you reach your goal every time

- This is how you show customers you care about them every time

- This is how you eat right – recipes for a younger and healthier life
- Salespeople – this is how you use your technique in a better way
- Take care of yourself better like this
- Tips for you who are too ambitious
- Tips on how to work from home
- Tips on how you make your business card work better for you
- Exercise right for good health
- How about starting a smart new habit
- Win against time
- Do you dare to take risks or are you a chicken?
- More on how you prepare yourself for change
- Superior tips that will better prepare you for your next network meeting
- 10 things to do to make your company sexier
- 6 tips on how you get a lost customer back
- 8 tips on that difficult art of telling bad news to customers
- 9 tips on how you cooperate your way to success
- Work conflicts – How you come to an agreement at work
- How to handle complaints from customers – like a hero
- Does your company need to change in order to bring in more customers?
- The most important question to all of us salespeople
- One sentence is enough for you to meet your goals
- Improve your information material and sell more
- Negotiate like a pro

- Sales for you who don't like selling
- Have you fallen into a trap?
- The secret of how to make boring jobs fun
- Elevator presentations – your guide
- How good are you at accepting criticism?
- How to catch a customer who calls, but doesn't buy
- How to build a creative company
- How to prepare yourself for change
- How to stage a coup through advertisement
- How to research a customer before you meet them
- How to really tick off your customers
- How to collect points with customers
- How to write a lot better at work
- How to sell ideas successfully
- How much is your brand worth, really?
- Can someone love their customers?
- The art of brainstorming
- Constructive criticism – how you give criticism in a better way
- Presentation speeches that work
- Corporal tunnel – what you do
- Positioning – what do customers get from your company that they don't get from others?
- Product development – this is how you should think
- Project planning in a simple way
- Business reference – How you get new customers through your old customers
- Right and wrong at the lunch meeting

- Things to do when business is slow
- Seven simple rules in sales for everyone in the company (including you)
- Laugh every day – this is how you do it
- Write agreements
- Write offers
- Smart job rules for everyone
- How to make your boss love you
- How to get customers to call you back
- How to get ideas on new products and services
- How to mingle right
- Tips on buying a new computer
- Service sales – 6 ways to measure up to your bigger competitors
- "The customer is always right" – and other babble
- Business angels – do they exist?
- To choose your business economy software
- How to choose an accountant – tips and advice
- The effective meeting
- Questions you should ask an investor
- Company financing – how it works
- Work for free – not your cup of tea?
- Cash flow – how you get a good cash flow
- Liquid budget – how to make one
- Recession tips
- Project budgeting – this is how you should be thinking
- Result budget – this is how you do it
- How you get a bank loan to your company

- What you need to know about book keeping
- 10 tips on how to make your website more accessible to customers
- Watch out for fake search engine optimisation
- Advertise better with AdWords
- Know this before trusting a company that claims they can make you number 1 on Google
- Keep old customers (and get new ones) with a newsletter
- Marketing through blogging – good or bad?
- More effective emailing
- One sentence that makes your company top of the class
- Number one on Google – That's not enough
- More visitors to your website – how you get them
- Are you losing money on emailing?
- Make your website more accessible to your visitors
- Make your site the best in the business
- Get higher rankings on search engines
- An action plan for those who don't have a website yet
- An action plan for those who already have a website
- An action plan for those who want to succeed on the internet
- Is your site collecting dust – This is how you make it fresh again
- How your site can become interesting to link to
- How you build a list of email addresses
- How you get others to want to link to your site
- How you make a good website
- How you know when you are a real internet nerd

- How you write on the web – a fast course on how you catch readers
- Here are the reasons why you'll want to start a newsletter
- Climb higher on search engines
- Will your internet shop bring in an income – test it yourself
- Buy a web shop – tips and advice
- The solution to abandoned shopping carts in your web shop
- Marketing with social networks
- More traffic to your site – how you do it
- About your site – read the article only after your vacation
- Planning a site – how you do it
- Policy for emailing
- A quick course on how to cure bad sales on your site
- Start an electronic newsletter
- Answer emails – or lose customers
- Visibility on the net – tips
- This is how you get visitors to buy more
- This is how you get visitors to stay longer = buy more
- This is how you get your internet customers to trust you
- This is how you make your site fantastic for everyone
- This is how you get more customers to your website
- This is how you create a more profitable business plan for the internet
- This is how customers test you on the internet
- This is how you increase sales on your site
- Sell more on the internet – tips and advice

- Websites that sell – how you do it
- Tips on Google's advertisement programme
- Three simple ways to lift your internet sales
- Think about your website correctly – Sit back and watch the customers buy
- What is a search engine really?
- Why do the customers not buy from your website?
- What you'll gain by having a website for your company
- Viral marketing – smart for you
- Web developing for you – concrete tips
- Increase your internet sales – how to brag correctly on the net

So grab a cup of coffee and get to work.

Notes

The Harriman House
small business library

www.harriman-house.com/categories/business

The Harriman House
small business library

www.harriman-house.com/categories/business

Lightning Source UK Ltd.
Milton Keynes UK
UKOW05f0345120517
300994UK00010B/179/P